A MEMORIAL

OF

EDWARD EVERETT,

FROM

THE CITY OF BOSTON.

BOSTON:
PRINTED BY ORDER OF THE CITY COUNCIL.
MDCCCLXV.

COMPILED BY J. M. BUGBEE,
THE MAYOR'S CLERK.

PRINTED BY J. E. FARWELL & COMPANY,
PRINTERS TO THE CITY.

THIS volume has been prepared, under the direction of a Committee of the City Council, for the purpose of preserving, in a permanent form, some of the numerous tributes of respect to the memory of EDWARD EVERETT, whose great accomplishments and unsurpassed eloquence were always devoted to the cause of good morals, to the elevation of the human race, and to creating in the hearts of his countrymen " THE LOVE OF LIBERTY PROTECTED BY LAW."

CONTENTS.

6   CONTENTS.

MEMOIR OF EDWARD EVERETT.

Edward Everett was born in Dorchester, Norfolk County, near Boston, on the 11th of April, 1794.* His father, Rev. Oliver Everett, had resigned the ministry of the New South Church, in Boston, in 1792, and removed to Dorchester, where he spent the remainder of his life. On his father's side Mr. Everett was descended from Richard Everett, or Everard, of Dedham, one of the early settlers in New-England, who is said by tradition to have been a soldier in the Low Countries. His mother was Lucy Hill, daughter of Alexander Sears Hill of Boston, and Mary Richey, and granddaughter of Alexander Hill, a merchant of Boston through the greater part of a long life. On both sides Mr. Everett was descended from ancestors almost all of whom were of the first Puritan emigration. His maternal grandmother, Mary Richey, was born in Philadelphia. His grandfather, Alexander Sears Hill, graduated at Harvard College in 1764, and died in 1771.

---

* In the preparation of this sketch, we have in some passages availed ourselves of a careful article published in the *Boston Daily Advertiser*, the day after Mr. Everett's death.

Rev. Oliver Everett, the father of Edward Everett, was the minister of the New South Church, in Boston, from 1782 to 1792, when, with failing health, he retired from the ministry. He was appointed Judge of the Circuit Court in 1799, and is sometimes spoken of as Judge Everett in the contemporary journals. He died on the 19th of November, 1802, and, in the spring of 1803, his widow, with her large young family removed to Boston. Edward Everett was then a boy of nine years of age, and since that time to his death he has been nearly connected, by residence or by official duty, with this town. His mother's residence at that time was in the street then known as Proctor's Lane, now the eastern part of Richmond Street. He was placed at school at the reading and writing schools in North Bennet Street, under the care of Master Ezekiel Little and Master John Tileston. At this " double school," in 1804, he received a Franklin Medal. In that year his mother removed her residence to a house now standing in Richmond Street, and on the death of her grandfather, Mr. Hill, removed again to a house in the upper part of Newbury Street, now Washington Street, nearly opposite the head of Essex Street. About this time Mr. Everett's regular preparation for college was begun, and he was sent to a private school, kept by Mr. Ezekiel Webster, of New Hampshire, a gentleman, says Mr. Everett himself, " of eminent talent and great worth, well entitled to be remembered for his own sake, but better known as the elder brother of Mr. Daniel Webster." On one occasion, during his brother's absence,

Mr. Daniel Webster took charge of the school for a week. It was thus that an acquaintance began, which afterwards ripened into the closest regard. Mr. Webster himself says of it, [July 21, 1852,] :

" We now and then see stretching across the heavens a clear, blue, cerulean sky, without cloud, or mist, or haze. And such appears to me our acquaintance, from the time when I heard you for a week recite your lessons in the little schoolhouse in Short Street to the date hereof." —

Few things, probably, were less in the thought of either, in that schoolhouse, than that the boy, as Governor of Massachusetts, would one day sign the commission of his teacher as Senator of the United States, or, at a later day, succeed him in the State Department.

In 1805 he was sent to the Latin Grammar School, then temporarily under the charge of Mr. Samuel Cooper Thacher, who soon afterwards left it in the charge of Mr. William Biglow. At this school, his classmates, as named in its own Catalogue, were William Turell Andrews, Samuel Blagge, John Borland, Charles Pelham Curtis, Nathaniel Langdon Frothingham, Benjamin Daniel Greene, Alba Hayward, George Edward Head, Harrison Gray Otis, William Parke, Edward Reynolds, William Smith, Solomon Davis Townsend, Benjamin Lincoln Weld, with two boys named Simpson whose other names are not given. At this school, in 1806, he received another Franklin Medal. In the same year he was sent to Exeter Academy, then under the charge of Dr. Benjamin Abbot, with the assistance of Nathan Hale and

Alexander H. Everett, Edward Everett's older brother. Here he remained till he was fitted for Harvard College, which he entered in the summer of 1807.

He graduated in 1811, and entered immediately on the study of Divinity, under the direction of President Kirkland, acting, at the same time, as Latin Tutor. In 1813 he was invited to become the minister of the Brattle Square Church, in Boston, and resumed his residence here. He was ordained on the 9th Feb., 1814.

In 1815 he was called by the government of Harvard College to the chair of the Greek Professorship, then recently established by Mr. Samuel Eliot. Accepting their invitation, he made his first visit to Europe to prepare for his new duties, and, in company with Mr. George Ticknor, went at once to Göttingen, they being among the first Americans to resort to a German university. Returning to America in 1819, after a long course of study and travel, he entered upon his professorship, where he gave, in the next four years, an impulse to the study of Greek literature in America which is not yet lost.

In 1822, while a professor at Cambridge, he married Charlotte Gray, daughter of the late Hon. Peter Chardon. Brooks. By this marriage he had three sons and four daughters. Four of these children are not now living. One of the daughters died soon after her birth. Grace Webster Everett, named for the wife of Hon. Daniel Webster, died in her ninth year. Anne Gorham Everett, who grew to womanhood, and shewed at an early age many of the traits of character and genius which distinguished her father, died in London, Oct. 18, 1854. Dr.

Edward Brooks Everett, who graduated at Cambridge in 1850, died November 5, 1861, leaving two children, Edward and Louisa Adams, by his wife, Helen Cordis, daughter of Benjamin Adams, Esq. of this city.

The children who survive Mr. Everett are Charlotte Brooks Wise, wife of Captain Henry Augustus Wise, of the United States Navy; Henry Sidney Everett, who graduated at Harvard College in 1855, now Major in the Volunteer Army of the United States, — and William Everett, who graduated at Harvard College in 1859, and took the degree of B. A. at the University of Cambridge, England, in 1862.

Mr. Everett was elected to Congress, at the election in 1824, from the Middlesex district, and, leaving his academic pursuits, entered upon a new and more public career as a statesman. He took his seat in the House of Representatives in 1825, as a supporter of Mr. Adams, and served there for ten years. He was at once appointed to the Committee on Foreign Affairs. To the foreign relations of the country, therefore, he gave especial attention, — but his interest was not limited to them. These years were marked by discussions on the most important interests in our legislation, and in many of these discussions he took a leading place. He served in Congress through Mr. Adams's administration, and part of that of General Jackson's.

In 1835 Mr. Everett was elected Governor of Massachusetts, and held that office for the four years following. His official term was a period of unusual interest in the history of the State. The Board of Education was then organized, the Normal Schools founded, the State subscription to the stock of the Western Railroad was made; and the division of the surplus revenue of the United States presented a unique question of State policy.

Losing his reëlection by a single vote in 1839, Mr. Everett, thus released from public duty, sailed for Europe the second time, in June 1840, with his family, and passed a winter in Italy. General Harrison's election, however, brought his political friends into favor, and Mr. Everett was appointed Minister at the Court of St. James. The questions relating to the Northeastern Boundary, the fisheries, the Caroline, the Creole, the case of McLeod, and other matters of dispute, were then at their most critical stage. Mr. Webster's intimate knowledge of the powers and qualifications of his friend gave the latter full scope for unfettered action; and never, it is safe to say, was a difficult diplomatic duty discharged with more judgment, delicacy, and grace. Multiplied marks of respect, — among which we may name only the honorary degrees conferred upon him by the Universities of Oxford, Cambridge, and Dublin, — testified the appreciation of the cultivated public opinion of England; and many personal friendships, with men of the highest position in society or in letters, remained until his last moment as the memorials of this period of his life. We may add that, more than once during the present war, proposals to accept diplomatic responsibilities of a confidential nature have marked the recollection of his triumphs in this part of his career, by members of the present administration.

Returning home in 1846, Mr. Everett was recalled to academic life, by his Alma Mater, which in that year elected him President, to succeed the venerable Josiah Quincy. Holding this position for three years, Mr. Everett resigned it in 1849, and for some years remained in comparative retirement.

While still at Cambridge, he had given an impulse to a movement for a Public Library in Boston, and he no sooner left the presidency of the College than he addressed himself to its establishment on a generous scale. In a letter to the Mayor of the City of Boston, Hon. John P. Bigelow, he suggested the plan which has been steadily carried forward from that moment, and now exhibits a result of the greatest interest and value. Different suggestions had been offered with regard to such a library, but they had slept without action, until Mr. Everett proposed the scheme to the Mayor. Mr. Bigelow immediately made the first contribution in money towards this purpose, and Mr. Everett sketched out a plan for the conduct of the institution. He had, while in Cambridge, made a large gift of books to the city, as a part of the nucleus of such an institution. A Board of Trustees was appointed, of which he was the chairman, a position which he held until his death. This Board, in conjunction with the appropriate committees of the City Government, opened a library, temporarily, in 1852. Mr. Joshua Bates, the intimate and confidential friend of Mr. Everett, in the autumn of the same year, made the first of a series of magnificent pecuniary gifts to it. This institution differs from every

other large library in the country, in being a circulating library, from which every person resident in the
town may take books, without charge, so long as he
observes the regulations. Mr. Everett lived long enough
to witness the complete success of his plans and answer to his wishes in its operations. He justly considered it as essential in a system which aims at
universal education.

At the death of Mr. Webster, in October, 1852,
Mr. Everett was called by President Fillmore to the
Department of State.

During the few months that he was Secretary of
State, he had occasion, in the matter of the proposed
tripartite convention respecting Cuba, to leave upon
record a memorable token of the reach and vigor of
his policy in foreign affairs. The change of administration, however, withdrew him from office, and in 1853 he
took his seat in the United States Senate, as successor
of Hon. John Davis. His health, however, which had
for some years been impaired, had now almost given
way, under the pressure of his labors in the Cabinet.
His sufferings during that winter were intense. He
spoke against the repeal of the Missouri Compromise, — a measure which he has termed the Pandora's
box from which our ills have flowed, — but was compelled in May, 1854, to resign his seat; and this event
terminated his career in public office in the service of
the Nation, with a single memorable exception.

The great work which he performed in the next
four years, when, with infirm bodily powers, he labored

incessantly for the Mount Vernon Fund, is fresh in the minds of all. The sum collected by his efforts for this noble object was little less than one hundred thousand dollars, and his motives for undertaking such a task, recently alluded to in one of his own public speeches, will command admiration as long as his name shall be remembered: —

" After the sectional warfare of opinion and feeling reached a dangerous height, anxious if possible to bring a counteractive and conciliating influence into play; feeling that there was yet one golden chord of sympathy which ran throughout the land; in the hope of contributing something, however small, to preserve what remained, and restore what was lost of kind feeling between the two sections of the country, — I devoted the greater part of my time for three years to the attempt to give new strength in the hearts of my countrymen to the last patriotic feeling in which they seemed to beat in entire unison, — veneration and love for the name of Washington, and reverence for the place of his rest. With this object in view, I travelled thousands of miles, by night and by day, in midwinter and midsummer, speaking three, four, and five times a week, in feeble health, and under a heavy burden of domestic care and sorrow, and inculcating the priceless value of the Union in precisely the same terms from Maine to Georgia and from New York to St. Louis."

The single exception alluded to, in which Mr. Everett once more discharged a high public function in the National service, was his fulfilment of the imposing charge given him by the people of Massachusetts, when they chose him their first Presidential Elector, in November, 1864. With this exception, his constant service as a Trustee of the Public Library of the city has been his only official duty. But in every walk of life he used his closing years in the service of his fellow-men. He had recently promised to deliver before the Dane Law School a course of lectures on International Law, and he was engaged in the preparation of these when he died.

The last occasion on which his voice was heard by his fellow-citizens in public, was at the meeting in Faneuil Hall on Monday, January 12, for the relief of the people of Savannah. To those who heard him on that occasion he seemed to exhibit more than his usual animation, and his face was free from the expression of subdued suffering which has too often marked it. Upon his return home, however, after a day of fatiguing engagements, he was obliged to summon his physician, and did not again leave his house, — suffering from a serious oppression of the lungs. He slept well through Saturday night, until shortly after four, when a sudden attack of an apoplectic nature ensued, which, in a few minutes, proved fatal. He died on the 15th of January, 1865, in the seventy-first year of his age.

ORDER

OF THE

PRESIDENT OF THE UNITED STATES.

DEPARTMENT OF STATE, WASHINGTON, January 15, 1865.

The President directs the undersigned to perform the painful duty of announcing to the people of the United States that Edward Everett, distinguished not more by learning and eloquence than by unsurpassed and disinterested labors of patriotism at a period of political disorder, departed this life at four o'clock this morning. The several Executive departments of the Government will cause appropriate honors to be rendered to the memory of the deceased, at home and abroad, wherever the national name and authority are acknowledged.

WM. H. SEWARD.

PROCEEDINGS IN THE CITY COUNCIL.

IN THE BOARD OF ALDERMEN.

A SPECIAL meeting of the Board of Aldermen was held on Monday, January 16, in response to a call by his Honor the Mayor, for the purpose of taking appropriate notice of the death of Mr. Everett.

The Mayor, on taking the chair, submitted the following communication : —

To THE HONORABLE THE CITY COUNCIL : —

GENTLEMEN : Yesterday, Sabbath morning, January 15, the Honorable Edward Everett was suddenly summoned by the Great Disposer of Events to finish his course on earth, and to enter upon the happiness of an immortal existence. The sober cares of God's holy day were sanctified by the hallowing influence of this sad event, and our community, which had been so long blessed by his presence, felt that they had sustained a loss which never can be filled by this generation.

I have deemed it my duty to order the bells of the city churches to be tolled, to announce to our inhabitants the death of their most distinguished citizen, and I have called you together at this unusual hour that you may take such measures as your own hearts and the proprieties of this solemn occasion may suggest.

Mr. Everett, through his long and honorable career, has been strongly identified with the reputation of Boston; and although his great talents and splendid accomplishments have often been at the service of the nation and the commonwealth, yet his dearest interests have been concentrated upon the community in which his home was chosen, and which depended upon him for advice and assistance in every great emergency and in all good works.

Boston never had a citizen who responded with more alacrity to her demands. He was ever ready to serve her in official relations, or on those more informal occasions, which were graced by his eloquence and power. His pen and tongue, whenever wanted, were devoted to her service and honor, and his highest happiness, I believe, was in ministering to the welfare of her people.

Commencing his public education in Boston, when nine years of age, as a pupil in the Eliot School, at the North End, where, in 1804, he received his first Franklin medal, he devoted a portion of the latter years of his great life to the care of the Public Library, acting, from its organization until his death, as the President of the Board of Trustees.

Faneuil Hall, so often the scene where the inspiration of his powerful and impassioned eloquence stirred the hearts of our people, witnessed his last intellectual effort; and his closing speech, before a popular assembly, was, by a wise Providence, ordained to be a pathetic and patriotic appeal in behalf of the suffering inhabitants of the city of Savannah. It was a grand and appropriate termination to a life of unselfish patriotism and distinguished public service.

His merits as a statesman, a scholar, and a philanthropist were acknowledged throughout the civilized world. We, who were drawn nearer to him in local matters, knew how to appreciate him as a citizen, as a man true in all the relations of social and domestic life, and one whose commanding influence was always brought to bear on the side of religion and morals, who was an example to youth, and a prompter of noble deeds to those in riper years.

Mr. Everett's memory will ever be cherished with pride by Bostonians, as one who has added to the fame of the city which he loved; and I have no doubt you will agree with me that, as he shared to so large an extent our admiration and respect while living, so he should be suitably remembered by the Municipal Government now that he is gone.

As the representatives of the people, it is our duty in their behalf to testify in some form our sense of the bereavement we have sustained by his death; and your action is respectfully invoked for such measures as may be proper, and which will comport with the dignity and character of the occasion. He has left no contemporary as his equal, and his name will be honored through many generations as a good and great man.

F. W. LINCOLN, Jr., Mayor.

4

Alderman Clapp thereupon offered the following preamble and resolutions : —

Whereas, in the ripeness of his years, and in the full possession of his great intellect, the Honorable Edward Everett has fallen by the hand of death, — taken from a field of usefulness boundless as his own love for his native country, — therefore it becomes us, in behalf of the City of Boston, to place on our records an expression of the grief which pervades all hearts, in a community realizing the great loss which the nation, the state, and the city sustained, when the immortal spirit of the statesman, patriot, and Christian broke from its earthly tenement for its journey through eternity.

Resolved, That the City Council of Boston, feeling a deep sense of obligation to the deceased for his invaluable services to its local institutions, and recognizing in his public life — almost without a parallel for the varied positions of trust which he has held at home and abroad — those elements of true greatness which are rarely combined in one man, do most sincerely unite in acknowledging that in every walk of life his nobility of character gave him a claim to our admiration, while the monuments of his literary ability and philanthropic effort will keep his memory sacred throughout all time.

Resolved, That the sympathy of the City Council be tendered to the bereaved family, in this the hour of their great affliction. There is consolation in the thought that it pleased God, in his goodness, to prolong the life of his servant, that he might prove, in the darkest hour of our history, a bright and shining light.

Resolved, That His Honor the Mayor be requested to call a meeting of the citizens, at Faneuil Hall, on Wednesday, at noon, that a public expression of the great loss sustained by this community may be a tribute of respect to the memory of the deceased.

Resolved, That a joint special committee of the two branches of the City Council be appointed, to express to the family the desire of the city to take such part in the funeral ceremonies as may be appropriate.

Resolved, That the committee be also empowered to make all arrangements for such other tokens of respect to the deceased as may be deemed due to his exalted fame.

Alderman Tyler spoke briefly in support of the resolutions, after which they were unanimously adopted, the members rising in their places.

Aldermen Tyler, Messinger, and Dana were appointed on the committee, on the part of the Board, to take charge of the funeral ceremonies.

Adjourned.

IN THE COMMON COUNCIL.

A SPECIAL meeting of the Common Council was also held on Monday, at 12 o'clock, M. to take action in concurrence with the Board of Aldermen in relation to the death of Mr. Everett. The President, William B. Fowle, Jr. Esquire, occupied the chair.

The communication of His Honor, the Mayor, and the resolutions of the Board, were received and read.

The President then spoke as follows : —

GENTLEMEN OF THE COMMON COUNCIL : —

It is rarely our fortune, in deploring the loss of a distinguished and valued citizen, to be able with our grief to combine so many truly pleasurable emotions. A retrospective view of the life of Edward Everett brings with it peculiar satisfaction. Endowed by Providence with an intellect rarely if ever surpassed, that intellect has been employed by him in single, honest effort for the true good of his country, and in promoting the welfare of his fellow-men.

Especially have the citizens of Boston felt his influence, and gloried in his intellect. To him, before all others, have we ever looked, in time of trouble, for counsel and advice, and at such times he has ever proved a pillar of strength and wisdom.

We mourn our loss; yet in our grief we thank a kind Providence that his great intellect was spared to the last, and that to the latest moment his usefulness was unimpaired.

The resolutions passed unanimously, the members rising.

The following members were appointed to join the committee of the Board: Clement Willis, Granville Mears, Jonas Fitch, John P. Ordway, and Benjamin F. Stevens. On motion, the President of the Council was added to this committee.

On motion of Mr. Stebbins of Ward 10, it was voted that the Clerk be authorized to send a copy of the resolutions passed, and the addresses of His Honor the Mayor and of the President of the Common Council, to the family of the deceased.

Adjourned.

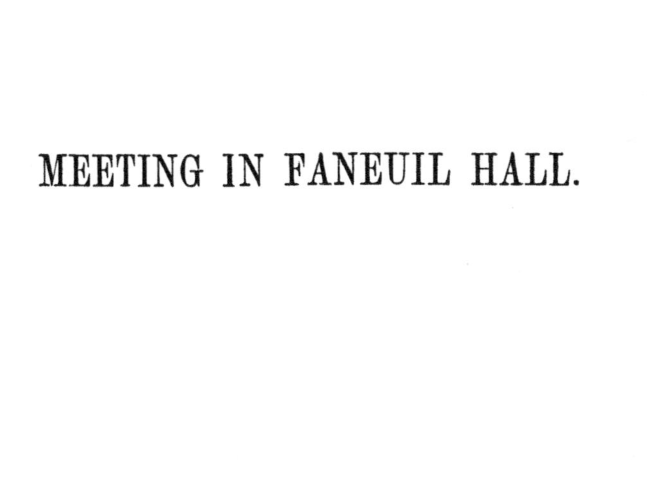

MEETING IN FANEUIL HALL.

MEETING IN FANEUIL HALL.

By invitation of His Honor the Mayor, a number of the prominent citizens of Boston met at the City Hall on Monday afternoon, January 16, for the purpose of consulting upon arrangements for a meeting in Faneuil Hall. It was decided to hold the meeting on Wednesday, January 18, 1865, at noon. The following Committees were appointed: —

On Organization: George B. Upton, J. Huntington Wolcott, Edward S. Tobey, Otis Norcross, and George C. Richardson. *On Resolutions:* Samuel H. Walley, George S. Hillard, Rev. S. K. Lothrop, George W. Bond, and H. P. Kidder.

The following notice was published in the newspapers: —

MAYOR'S OFFICE, CITY HALL,
BOSTON, January 16, 1865.

TO THE CITIZENS OF BOSTON: —

In conformity with a resolve passed this day by the City Council, the citizens of Boston are invited to assemble in Faneuil Hall, on Wednesday, January 18, at 12 o'clock, for the purpose of taking such measures as may be deemed appropriate to express their sense of the loss the nation and this community have sustained by the recent decease of their late eminent fellow citizen, Edward Everett.

F. W. LINCOLN, JR.

At the hour designated in the above notice, the citizens of Boston convened in Faneuil Hall, — attracted there, as their appearance would indicate, through no idle curiosity, but through a desire to testify, by their presence, to the sorrow which pervaded the community. The darkened hall, the symbols of mourning upon the walls, the sad and subdued expression of the assemblage, combined to make the scene remarkably impressive.

At twelve o'clock, Mr. George B. Upton came forward upon the platform, and read, as the report of the Committee on Organization, the following list of officers for the meeting: —

PRESIDENT,

His Honor, F. W. LINCOLN, Jr.

VICE-PRESIDENTS,

Chief Justice G. T. Bigelow,	J. Thomas Stevenson,
Charles G. Loring,	Charles G. Greene,
George Ticknor,	Rt. Rev. J. B. Fitzpatrick,
John C. Gray,	Thomas Aspinwall,
Robert C. Winthrop,	Silas Peirce,
Rev. G. W. Blagden,	George W. Lyman,
James Savage,	J. Z. Goodrich,
Stephen Fairbanks,	Dr. George Hayward,
Rt. Rev. Manton Eastburn,	Joseph T. Bailey,
Charles Wells,	Albert Fearing,
J. G. Palfrey,	Josiah Quincy,
David Sears,	James W. Paige,
Dr. James Jackson,	Patrick Donahoe,
Francis C. Lowell,	James Read,
William B. Reynolds,	

SECRETARIES,

William W. Greenough,	Patrick T. Jackson,
Edwin P. Whipple,	J. Tisdale Bradlee.

Mayor Lincoln took the chair, and prayer was offered by Rev. S. K. Lothrop, D.D., Pastor of the Brattle Street Church. The Mayor then addressed the meeting as follows : —

FELLOW-CITIZENS : —

The official position which it is my fortune to occupy brings with it, through your courtesy, the distinguished honor of presiding over the deliberations of this assembly.

The sad event which has called us together has cast a shadow over all the land, but its deepest gloom is naturally felt in this community; and this venerable hall, clad in its mourning habiliments, feebly represents the grief which oppresses all our hearts. The opening dawn of the first day of the week closed the earthly career of our foremost man ; and we are assembled, before his body has received its funeral rites, and has been " committed to the holy mystery of the ground," to do honor to his memory, and to express our sense of the bereavement we have sustained by his death.

We have met, fellow-citizens, to dwell for a while on the merits of one who has so often led our thoughts in contemplation of the distinguished dead. It is hard for us to realize, especially within these walls, that those eloquent lips are dumb, and that he, too, is gone, never more to stand on this platform, before a waiting multitude eager to hear those words of wisdom and cheer, which dropped like manna when he spoke. It has been my great privilege, for a number of years past, to be a personal witness, on public occasions, or in more private ways, to Mr. Everett's zeal and devotion to the welfare of this community, and his stanch and unswerving loyalty to his native land.

His presence was a benediction. The world is better that he has lived in it; and his memory will be one of those rich treasures which can never be taken away from his countrymen. Boston, as his home, was ever dear to him. He was interested in its most trivial concerns, while his comprehensive mind extended and took delight in those vast affairs which constitute our strength and character as a nation.

It does not become me, in this presence, surrounded as I am by the talented and gifted of the community, to speak to you of his genius, and of the rich fruits of his noble career. The consummate ability which distinguished his public efforts, and the dignity and grace of his private life, will be discoursed upon by those who, in fitting words, can do justice to such topics. My only duty is, with your indulgence, to conduct in some degree the proceedings of the meeting, and by my official presence, in an humble way, to be the representative of the City of Boston on this occasion.

Hon. Samuel H. Walley was introduced, and read, without prefatory remark, the following series of resolutions : —

It having pleased Almighty God, in the exercise of his all-wise Providence, to remove by death our fellow-citizen, Edward Everett, whose decease occurred at his residence in this city, on Sunday morning, January 15, 1865, in the seventy-first year of his age; therefore,

Resolved, That we bow with humble acquiescence to the will of God, knowing that the Judge of all the earth will do right; that all men and all events are at his disposal; and that it becomes us to believe that he knows infinitely better than we do, or can, the most appropriate season for the departure of each individual, however lowly, or however highly exalted, from time to eternity.

Resolved, That we are bound by every sense of obligation of which we are capable to acknowledge with gratitude the goodness of God, in granting to our community so rich a gift as we all feel was contained in the natural endowments, the rare opportunities, the conscientious nature, the extensive influence, and the protracted life of our departed friend.

Resolved, That in the death of Mr. Everett, not alone his family, not alone the city where he lived, the commonwealth to which he belonged, the bleeding and distracted nation of which he was an essential part, — not alone all of these, but the world of letters and of learning, the world of eloquence and refined culture, the world of science and of profound scholarship, the cause of humanity at large and of human freedom in particular, the cause of Christian morality and of humble, unostentatious Christian life and conversation, —

mourn the loss of a bright, inflexible, and consistent exemplar.

Resolved, That in tracing the varied and eventful life of him whose decease we this day mourn, we are forcibly reminded of its fitting commencement and close. His earliest strains of eloquence, ere he had reached the age of manhood, having sounded forth from the pulpit to crowded audiences, who hung upon his lips with thrilling interest; while his almost dying words were an eloquent plea to his fellow-citizens to give heed to the teachings of Holy Writ — "If thine enemy hunger, feed him; if he thirst, give him drink."

Resolved, That in reviewing the claims to our respect and admiration furnished by the life of our friend, kindly continued beyond threescore and ten, we are forcibly reminded of the fact that, unlike most men, his severest trial was to satisfy himself, as he was always his own great rival, — never failing to meet the expectations of his friends, but never satisfying his own demands upon himself. And with all his native modesty and diffidence, at times mistaken, by those who did not know the workings of his heart and his true nature, for coldness of manner, it was apparent to all careful observers that each step in his progress through life seemed to be onward and upward, — not always pleasing all men, for then he would have been of little worth, but always acting from a high sense of conscientious obligation to the Giver of his splendid talents.

Resolved, That while we are at a loss which most

to admire of all the rare endowments of the departed, his course may well be likened to the sun in the heavens, — rising full-orbed in a cloudless sky, shining brightly as it approached meridian, and continuing with undiminished splendor until its setting hour; when, still full-orbed and large, undimmed and in unclouded light, it quietly sank below the horizon. Thus did he of whom we speak; constantly adding to his knowledge, that he might instruct the more from the rich store-house of his cultivated mind; and went forward in life instructing the people in the church, in the college, in the senate, at the foreign court, and in the cabinet at home, till wearied of the vexations of political strife, and with impaired health he sought rest in retirement. But with renewed health he rose again to view, more bright than ever, and, with a zeal and a power unsurpassed, labored to save his country from civil war, by commending to North and South the example and counsels of Washington; and failing in this effort, — finding his flag assailed and his country imperilled, — with a magnanimity and self-forgetfulness, and a power of eloquence worthy of all praise and imitation, he devoted all his energies to the single work of saving his country, and reuniting it upon a secure and righteous basis, with no stripe erased, no star blotted from its flag, no stain upon its fair escutcheon. It was in this, the last epoch of his eventful life, that he shone out full-orbed, and secured an abiding place for the record of his fame on the imperishable scroll of a nation's gratitude.

Resolved, That a life so full of well-directed, industrious effort, coupled with powers of a high order,—a life marked strongly throughout, but brilliantly at its close, by deeds of unselfish patriotism, deserves to be held up no less for the imitation of posterity than for the commendation of contemporaries; and in order to associate in the minds of future beholders the lineaments of his person with the history of his greatness, it is expedient that a statue should be erected in honor of Edward Everett.

Resolved, That a committee of fifty citizens be appointed by the Chair, in accordance with the previous resolve.

Resolved, That while we do not presume to trespass on the sacred retirement of domestic grief, called forth by the loss of one who was so admirable in all the domestic relations,—we may be permitted to tender our heartfelt sympathy to the family of the deceased, in this hour of sudden and heavy sorrow; and at the same time to point them to the abundant consolations afforded by such a close to such a life.

Resolved, That a copy of these resolutions be forwarded by the officers of this meeting to the family of Edward Everett.

The President then introduced Hon. Charles G.. Loring, whose remarks were as follows : —

Mr. Chairman and Fellow-Citizens : —

In obedience to the request of the authorities under whose auspices this meeting is assembled, and the impulses of friendship and admiration for the illustrious man whose death it is designed to commemorate, I am here to speak to you of the decease of Edward Everett. But what shall I say? The theme is so full and exhaustless that I know not where to begin, and if I could rightly begin, I should not know where to end. The simple announcement that Edward Everett is dead so fills the minds of such an audience of fellow-townsmen and friends with thickly crowding recollections and emotions, that the mere utterance of the mournful truth seems to be all that is needed to awaken the most affecting remembrances of his virtues, and of his services for ourselves and our country, and to inspire each heart with its own most fitting eulogium.

A few brief weeks only have passed since he stood upon this platform to vindicate, what seemed to him and to most of us, the great cause of our beloved country. The sounds of your plaudits upon his appearance, and of your enthusiastic approbation of his address, seem to be still ringing in my ears, and to be reverberating from these walls; a few brief days only have gone since he again stood here, in eloquent and effective appeals to your benevolence, your magnanimity, and your patriotism, in behalf of the famishing poor of Savannah. It seems almost impossible to bring home to our hearts the reality that we are never again to listen to his words of counsel, to his bursts of patriotic enthusiasm, or his touching appeals in behalf of downtrodden humanity; and that these same walls are now so soon echoing to lamentations over his bier.

Upon the former of those occasions it was remarked that when the time should come, which it was trusted might be far distant, for contemplating the monument which his life and services would constitute in the history of his country, when the eye shall have lingered in admiration upon the entablatures commemorative of his character, his scholarship, his eloquence, and his statesmanship, it would at last rest with still fonder delight upon that which shall tell of his patriotism, when, Samson-like, bursting the withes of old political associations, he threw himself, heart and hand, into the cause of his country, to save her, if possible, from the perils with which she was surrounded. How soon, alas! has this prophecy become history.

Proud, as we justly may be, of his varied learning, his matchless oratory, his world-wide reputation as a scholar and a statesman; and pleasant as it might be to dwell upon all that he has accomplished for letters and art and science, and the fame of his native land; how instinctively, nay, how almost exclusively, we now turn to contemplate his noble patriotism; the devotion of his great powers and generous heart to the service of his country. How much dearer to us is Edward Everett the patriot, than he ever could have been if only Edward Everett the scholar, the statesman, and the orator, although standing without a rival. His patriotism, however, though fervent, was not marred by any unjust disparagement of those who, seeking their country's welfare, differed from him in their judgment of the best means of securing it. While no one could question the sincerity and purity of his motives, he was wholly above any ungenerous distrust of theirs.

When the family of a great and good man stand around his grave, it is not the termination of his career of intellectual achievement, or of future opportunity for its triumphs, that causes the tear to drop upon the coffin lid, but the thought that the wise counsellor, the noble exemplar, the strong protector, and the loving friend is gone, and that the places which knew him shall know him no more forever. So now, fellow-citizens, we, — united as we feel ourselves to be in patriotic friendship, man to man, as never before, in this mighty struggle for national life, — gather around the bier of Edward Everett in sympathizing grief, that we can no longer be guided by his counsels, encouraged by his patriotism, and sustained by his intellectual strength and influence. Nor do we bend over it alone. The wretched sufferers in Tennessee, whom his efforts have so effectually aided to rescue from starvation, and other horrors consequent upon a fiendish persecution, — the destitute mingled friends and foes of Savannah, for whom he so earnestly and successfully pleaded here a few days ago, — the last effort of those eloquent lips now cold in death, — the exultant freedman, the cowering refugee, the noble soldiers in the hospitals, — all of whose causes he has upheld and promoted by his eloquence and his toils, with the patriots of every name throughout the land, all are heartfelt mourners with us to-day.

This is not the time or the occasion for an enumeration or an analysis of the intellectual powers and traits of character of our friend; otherwise it were easy and delightful to trace his career, for their illustration, from the remarkably precocious development of his literary powers in boyhood to their maturity in manhood and old age; to follow him from the college, in which he was graduated with the highest honors, to the tutor's chair, to the pulpit, the professorship, the editorship of the *North American Review*, to the halls of Congress, in both branches, to the gubernatorial chair of this Commonwealth, to the Cabinet as Minister of State, to the chief of our foreign diplomatic missions, to the Presidency of Harvard College, and other stations of duty and honor, in all of which he was distinguished by unsurpassed ability and unswerving fidelity; to his glorious enterprise for uniting the hearts of the people throughout the land in the knowledge of the character and principles of the Father of his Country, and in the establishment of Mount Vernon as the monument of a nation's reverence and gratitude; and, finally, to that widely diffused and vast personal influence which he obtained throughout our country, and which he has so signally devoted to her service in this her hour of need. But we are not here to celebrate his achievements, or glory in his fame. The time is not distant, we may trust, when the erection of a suitable statue to his memory shall give opportunity for such a record. We are here now, in justice to ourselves, that we may unite in testifying to our sense of his worth, and our just appreciation of the loss which this community especially, and our whole country, has sustained in his death. I heartily second the resolutions.

Hon. Robert C. Winthrop was the next speaker. He addressed the meeting in the following words: —

I hardly know, fellow-citizens and friends, I hardly know either how to speak or how to be silent here to-day. I dare not trust myself to any off-hand, impulsive utterance on such a theme. And yet I cannot but feel how poor and how inadequate to the occasion is the best preparation which I am capable of making. I am sincerely and deeply sensible how unfitted I am, by emotions which I should in vain attempt to restrain, for meeting the expectations and the demands of such an hour, or for doing justice to an event which has hardly left a heart unmoved, or an eye unmoistened, in our whole community. Most gladly would I still be permitted to remain a listener only, and to indulge a silent but heartfelt sorrow for the loss of so illustrious a fellow-citizen and so dear a friend.

I have so often been privileged to follow him on these public occasions of every sort, that I feel almost at a loss how to proceed without the encouragement of his friendly countenance and the inspiration of his matchless tones. I seem to myself to be still waiting for his ever-welcome, ever-brilliant lead. I find it all but impossible to realize the fact, that we are assembled here in Faneuil Hall, at a meeting at which whatever is most eloquent, whatever is most impressive, whatever is most felicitous and most finished, ought justly to be heard, and that Edward Everett is not here with us to say the first, the best, the all-sufficient word. I feel myself impelled to exclaim — and you will all unite with me in the exclamation —

> "Oh, for the sound of a voice that is still'd,
> And the touch of a vanished hand."

Certainly, my friends, I can find no other words to begin with, than those which he himself employed, when rising to speak in this hall on the death of that great statesman, whose birthday, by a strange but touching coincidence, we are so sadly commemorating to-day by this public tribute to his life-long friend and chosen biographer: "There is but one voice," said Mr. Everett of Daniel Webster, and certainly I may repeat it of himself to-day, "There is but one voice that ever fell upon my ear which could do justice to such an occasion. That voice, alas, we shall hear no more forever."

Yes, fellow-citizens, as a celebrated Roman historian said of the consummate orator of his own land and age, that to praise him worthily required the eloquence of Cicero himself, so we cannot fail to feel that full justice to the career and character of our American Cicero could only be rendered by the best effort of his own unequalled powers. It is hardly an exaggeration to say of him, that he has left behind him no one sufficient to pronounce his eulogy as it should be pronounced; no one, certainly, who can do for him all that he has done for so many others who have gone before him.

But, indeed, my friends, the event which has called us

together has occurred too suddenly, too unexpectedly, for
any of us to be quite prepared either for attempting or
for hearing any formal account of our departed friend's
career, or any cold analysis of his public or private character. There must be time for us to recover from the first
shock of so overwhelming a loss before his eulogy can be
fitly undertaken or calmly listened to. His honored remains are still awaiting those funeral rites in which our
whole community will so eagerly and so feelingly unite
to-morrow. The very air we are breathing at this moment
is still vocal and vibrating with his last public appeal. It
seems but an instant since he was with us on this platform,
pleading the cause of humanity and Christian benevolence
in as noble strains as ever fell from human lips. And no
one, I think, who had the privilege of hearing that appeal,
can fail to remember a passage, which did not find its way
into any of the printed reports, but which made a deep
impression on my own heart, as I stood on yonder floor a
delighted listener to one whom I could never hear too
often. It was the passage in which, in terms quite
unusual for him, and which seemed as if the shadow of
coming events were passing over his mind, he spoke of
himself as " an old man who had nothing but his lips left
for contributing to the public good." Nothing but his
lips left! Ah, my friends, what lips those were ! If ever
since the days of the infant Plato, of whom the story is
told, if ever since that age of cunning fable and of deep
philosophy with which he was so familiar, the Attic bees
have lighted upon any human lips, and left their persuasive honey there without a particle of their sting, it must

have been on those of our lamented friend. What lips they were! And what have they not accomplished since they were first opened in mature, articulate speech! What worthy topic have they not illustrated! What good and noble cause have they not advocated and adorned! On what occasion of honor to the living or to the dead, — at what commemoration of the glorious past — in what exigency of the momentous present — have those lips ever been mute? From what call of duty or of friendship, of charity or of patriotism, have they ever been withheld?

Turn to those three noble volumes of his works, and follow him in that splendid series of Orations which they contain — from the earliest at Cambridge, in which he pronounced that thrilling welcome to Lafayette a little more than forty years ago, down to that on the 4th of July, 1858, which he concluded by saying, that in the course of nature he should go to his grave before long, and he wished no other epitaph to be placed upon it than this: " Through evil report and through good report he loved his whole country: " — Follow him, I say, in his whole career as unfolded in those noble volumes — the best manual of American Eloquence — and then take up the record of those other Orations and Addresses which are still to be included in his collected works, the record of the last few years, as it is impressed upon the minds and hearts of every patriot in our land — with all its grand appeals for Mount Vernon and the memory of Washington, for the sufferers of East Tennesee, for the preservation of the Union, for the defence of the country against rebellion and treason, for the support of the National Administration agreeably to his own honest convictions of duty: Follow him, I say again, along the radiant pathway of that whole career, illuminated as it is from his earliest manhood to the last week of his life by the sparkling productions of his own genius, and then tell me, you who can, what cause of education or literature, what cause of art or industry, what cause of science or history, what cause of religion or charity, what cause of philanthropy or patriotism, has not been a debtor — a debtor beyond the power of payment — and, now alas! beyond the power of acknowledgment, — to his voice or to his pen! Who has ever more fairly won the title of "the golden-mouthed," since the sainted Chrysostom of old, than he who, by the music of his voice and the magic of his tongue, has so often coined his thoughts into eagles and turned his words into ingots, at one moment for the redemption of the consecrated home and grave of the Father of his Country, and at another for the relief of an oppressed and suffering people!

And who, my friends, as he reviews this marvellous career, can fail to remember how singularly applicable to him, in view of his earliest as well as of his later callings, are those words in which the immortal drama-tist has described the curious felicity and facility of speech, and the extraordinary versatility of powers, of one of the great princes and sovereigns of England: —

> " Hear him but reason in divinity,
> And, all-admiring, with an inward wish
> You would desire the king were made a prelate :
> Hear him debate of commonwealth affairs,

7

> You 'd say, it hath been all-in-all his study :
> List his discourse of war, and you shall hear
> A fearful battle rendered you in music :
> Turn him to any cause of policy,
> The Gordian knot of it he will unloose,
> Familiar as his garter ; that when he speaks,
> The air, a chartered libertine, is still,
> And the mute wonder lurketh in men's ears,
> To steal his sweet and honeyed sentences."

It is hardly too much to say of him that he established a new standard of American eloquence, that he was the founder of a new school of occasional oratory, of which he was at once the acknowledged master and the best pupil, and in which we were all proud to sit at his feet as disciples. Would that we had been better scholars! Would that, now that he has been snatched so suddenly from our sight, and as we follow him to the skies with our parting acclamations of admiration and affection, we could feel that there were some shoulders not wholly unworthy to wear, not altogether incapable of sustaining, his falling mantle !

I need not dwell for a moment, my friends, upon the details of his official life. We all remember his earlier and his later relations to the University to which he was so ardently attached, and which has ever counted him among its proudest ornaments. We all remember how long and how faithfully he served the State and the Nation in their highest departments at home and abroad. But public office was not necessary to his fame, and he never held his title to consideration at the precarious

tenure of public favor or popular suffrage. Office gave
no distinction to the man ; but the man gave a new distinction and a new dignity to every office which he held.
Everywhere he was the consummate scholar, the brilliant
orator, the Christian gentleman, — greater, even, as a private citizen than in the highest station to which he ever
was, or ever could have been called.

I need not dwell for a moment, either, my friends,
upon the purity and beauty of his daily life, upon his devotion to his family, his fidelity to his friends, his integrity as a man, his untiring willingness and eagerness to
do kind and obliging things for all who, reasonably or un-
reasonably, asked them at his hands, at any cost of time
or trouble to himself. I can never fail, certainly, to remember his countless acts of kindness to myself during a
friendship of thirty years. I do not forget that at least
once in my life I have differed from him on important
questions, and that recently; but I can honestly say that
there was no living man from whom I differed with a
deeper regret, or with a greater distrust of my own judgment. Nor can I fail to remember with inexpressible joy
at this hour, that within a week, I had almost said within
a day, after that difference was avowed and acted upon,
he reciprocated most kindly and most cordially an assurance, that our old relations of friendship and affection
should suffer no estrangement or interruption, and that
we would never distrust each other's sincerity or each
other's mutual regard. " I am not afraid," he wrote me,
" that we shall give each other cause of offence ; and we
will not let others put us at variance."

Fellow-Citizens: I knew not how to commence these imperfect and desultory remarks, and I know not how to close them. There is, I am sensible, much to console us in our bereavement, severe and sudden as it is. We may well rejoice and be grateful to God, that our illustrious and beloved friend was the subject of no lingering illness or infirmity, that he was permitted to die while in the full possession of his powers, while at the very zenith of his fame, and while he had a hold on the hearts of his countrymen such as even he had never before enjoyed. We may well rejoice, too, that his voice was last heard in advocating a measure of signal humanity which appealed to every heart throughout the land, and that he lived to see of the fruit of his lips and to be satisfied. I hold in my hand one of his last notes, — written on Thursday evening to our munificent and excellent fellow-citizen, Mr. William Gray, and which, in his own necessary and regretted absence, he has kindly permitted me to read: —

"SUMMER STREET, 12 Jan. 1865.

"*My dear Mr. Gray:* I am greatly obliged to you for sending me word of the success of the Savannah subscription. What a large-hearted, open-handed place we live in! It is on these occasions that I break the tenth commandment, and covet the wealth of you millionaires. I have been in bed almost ever since Monday, having narrowly escaped an attack of pneumonia. I had been in the court-house all the morning, and had to return to it for three hours in the afternoon to attend to a harassing arbitration case, and left Faneuil Hall with my extremities ice, and my lungs on fire. But in such a cause one is willing to suffer.

"Ever sincerely yours,

"EDWARD EVERETT."

This little note, my friends, in his own unmistakable and inimitable hand, written within two days of his death, shows clearly what thoughts were uppermost in that noble heart, before it so suddenly ceased to beat. In such a cause he was willing to suffer. In such a cause he was not unwilling to die.

But whatever consolation may be found in the circumstances of his death, or in the occupation of his last years, or months, or days, we still cannot but feel that no heavier public calamity could at this moment, if at any moment, have befallen our community. We cannot but feel that not Boston only, not Massachusetts only, not New England only, but our whole country, is called to deplore the loss of its most accomplished scholar, its most brilliant orator, its most valuable citizen. More and more, as the days and the years roll on, will that loss be perceived and felt by all who have known, admired, and loved him. The public proceedings of this day, the sad ceremonials of to-morrow, will find their place on the page of history. All the customary tributes of respect and gratitude to our lamented friend will at no distant day be completed. We shall hang his portrait on these hallowed walls in fit companionship with the patriot forms which already adorn them. We shall place a statue of him, in due time, I trust, on yonder terrace, not far from that of his illustrious and ever-honored friend. But neither portrait nor statue, nor funeral pomp, nor public eulogy, will have done for his memory, what he has done for it himself. The name and the fame of Edward Everett will in no way more surely be perpetuated than by the want which will be experienced, by the aching void which will be felt, on all our occasions of commemoration, on all our days of jubilee, on every literary anniversary, at every festive board, in every appeal for education, for charity, for country, in every hour of peril, in every hour of triumph, from the loss of that ever-ready, ever-welcome voice, which has so long been accustomed to say the best, the most appropriate, the most effective word, in the best, the most appropriate, the most effective manner. For nearly half a century no public occasion has ever seemed complete without his presence. By a thousand conspicuous acts of public service, by a thousand nameless labors of love, for young and old, for rich and poor, for friends and for strangers, he has rendered himself necessary — so far as any one human being ever can be necessary — to the welfare and the honor of the community in which he lived. I can find no words for the oppression I feel, in common, I am sure, with all who hear me, at the idea that we shall see his face and hear his voice no more. As I looked on his lifeless form a few hours only after his spirit had returned to God who gave it, — as I saw those lips which we had so often hung upon with rapture, motionless and sealed in death, — and as I reflected that all those marvellous acquisitions and gifts, that matchless memory, that exquisite diction, that exhaustless illustration, that infinite variety, which no age could wither and no custom stale, — that all, all were henceforth lost to us forever, I could only recall the touching lines which I remembered to have seen applied to the sudden death, not many years ago, of a kindred spirit of old England, — one of her greatest statesmen, one of his most valued friends —

> "Could not the grave forget thee, and lay low
> Some less majestic, less beloved head?
> Those who weep not for Kings shall weep for thee,
> And Freedom's heart grow heavy at thy loss!"

Hon. Alexander H. Bullock, then spoke as follows: —

MR. MAYOR AND FELLOW-CITIZENS: —

This place which welcomed him through so many years, this hour of noon in which he so often charmed and instructed us, the tones of his voice yet lingering here to plead a sublime charity, are better than the written or spoken words, with which you seek to encompass with mournful honors the name of our illustrious and departed citizen. And yet the ties of state, the pride of fellowship, the memory of services, bring us by instinct here to form the long train of those who lament this death, so unexpected, so timely. Our assembling is not to add honors to him who had won his own, but to testify in the general grief, that, born among us, living his life in the presence of us, placed by us in the highest positions with which we could invest him, he kept to the last, bright and electric the sympathies of the mutual relationship, so that when he passed away, we, above all others, felt the shock of the separation. He not only died among his kindred, but in the midst of a people who had made him especially their own. He was the contemporary of two generations in the State, but his mental activity, his increasing wisdom, his maturing fame, had made Mr. Everett, beyond the lot of most men, a brighter and more particular treasure to the second generation, than he had been to the first. The pall fell from heaven at the right moment. Never before had we respected him so greatly, never before had we esteemed him so tenderly, as when he died crowned with age that bore the emblems of youth, rich in renown that blended the splendor of manhood with the mellow lustre of later years, carrying to the portals of immortality that noble vindication of a long life which devotion to patriotism and philanthropy best furnishes as the closing scene.

This is not the time to pass in review the varied career of our lamented statesman and scholar. He *was* statesman and scholar in the highest sense, and he made the two characters reflect upon each other, that light and glory which, when blended, makes the life of a public man most radiant. Here in this mart of commerce I hold up his name in behalf of the retreats of the schools. His early academic success, which for example and fascination was the first and best our country has supplied, upon which he never turned an averted face, as men are accustomed too frequently to do in the rude turmoil of our politics, was a life-long and elemental power which he wielded in every sphere of his labors. He carried it from yonder shades into Congress; was never ashamed to use it there; never fell away from it, and rose upon it to the respect and admiration of his associates. No man from Eton or Oxford ever did more in this respect for the parliament of Great Britain, than he has done for ours. So Canning graced and delighted her Commons; so the ignorance of Castlereagh was more than once rebuked; so Pitt made a broad scholarship an instrument of power — a weapon for an onset. Our Canning produced the same effect by the scope and beauty of his example, though among older, more arrogant, more overpowering men, it was not in accord with his nature to lead in the positive attack. This was the bed whence blossomed the flowers of a large and enduring influence. Entering Congress in its palmiest period, and continuing there ten years, while its great Senators were wont to come into the House to listen to our Everett and Choate, it was fortunate for us that he so kept high the standard of debate, and so adorned the counsels of statesmanship, with the graces of learning and of eloquence, that when he came away to take the chair of our State at home, he left behind a treasured memory of cultured mastery for the State at the capitol. I know that Mr. Clay, listening to him for the first time, then thirty-five or six years of age, said to a bystander, " this is the acme of eloquence." Our Commonwealth cannot afford to forget her sons who have given her the first place in the Federal councils — who, opening a brilliant career for themselves, have illustrated her institutions and enlarged her capacity for beneficence. It has been our good fortune, to have had there a long line of such statesmen, which began with Ames, which found a complete representative in Everett. Each one has been a stimulation to the other. Mr. Choate once told me that while residing in Washington it was his pride to gather up the scattered traditions, floating through all that social life, of the forensic efforts of Webster; and who shall say how much his own transcendent idea may have been quickened by the magic of such rumor? Mr. Everett in the twelve years he served in the two houses, so far as I know, brought never to any discussion, a rhetorical treatment that would have done discredit to Burke, or Fox, or Romilly. Such attainment deserves our perpetual remembrance. It is among the enduring forces by which we may hope to influence greater States and greater numbers than our own in all after time.

From his academic and Congressional course Mr. Everett passed to the curule chair of Massachusetts. He held it in those dull times of peace, four years, while it furnished no deep excitements to his ambition. It was not a time or a place for special originations. The genius of that period was the genius of some improvement, but of more routine. And yet I conceive that he performed a good work for us, and for posterity, in his support of our grand State system existing already, and as the official patron of those greater and better plans of education and charity which make States immortal. It is now a quarter of a century since his administration terminated, and in the more conspicuous action which has since distinguished him on broader and more fertile fields of fame, that has been comparitively obscured. But it was an essential portion of his life. His record as chief magistrate is without blemish. He never lowered the dignity of state; he never called unworthy counsel around him; he left the office untarnished as he found it.

It does not comport with my purpose of brevity to detain you with reminiscences which belong to protracted address or stated biography. I regard as among the more striking services he has rendered, his connection at two periods with our foreign affairs. You remember how the advent of Mr. Webster to the Department of State found Mr. Everett in a foreign land, whither he had repaired for a scholar's travel and a scholar's solace. At the call of the President he accepted the credentials for the highest court of Europe. It was a critical period. History is too busy now with graver matters at home to have much space for that; but it was a critical epoch. The shadows of war frowned from the Canadas; the fires of the Caroline lighted up the frontier. We came out of the crisis without the stain of blood or the discolor of smoke upon our diplomatic robes. You may distribute the honors as you please among Webster, and Ashburton, and Everett, but he who stood our representative before the grandest court of the world, in constant correspondence and mutual counsel with his great friend at the capitol, cannot be overlooked in the impartial distribution.

About ten years later, he himself was called to the Department of State, which was vacant. It had been vacated by the death of Daniel Webster. It was a great vacancy, which no man could fill so well. Think a moment, to what statesmanship in diplomacy Mr. Everett succeeded. Have you sufficiently reflected, that great as Webster has been at the bar, and in the Senate, he was greater still at the august international tribunal, in the court of nations, before the juries of history? Such he proved himself to be. How, under Harrison, he asserted himself, and vindicated his country to unprecedented grandeur. How, in the case of the Caroline, he dramatized the literature of the international code by the elements of his conception and the majesty of his rhetoric. How, in the question of impressment, he settled all that Rush and those after him had left loose and unadjusted, by the memorable despatch, which has never received a reply and never can receive a refutation. How, in the Treaty of Washington, he drew those northeastern lines with the precision of science and with the power of destiny, that shall last forever. Mr. Everett succeeded to HIS chair, and carried with him the confidence of Massachusetts that he would prove equal to the exigency. The teacher had departed, but the disciple remained to complete his mission. It was a new era in his life; but he more than matched its necessities. By one comprehensive study, by one continuous and magnetic triumph of his pen, he raised what some of us thought the effete and demoralized administration of Fillmore, to the respect of a chivalrous people. His tri-partite letter, unique, original, and independent, justified our America upon a base exclusively her own. The philosophy of that letter was well then; it is better now. It is a quiver from which we may draw the weapons against any and every European intervention. Mr. Everett of the Cabinet of 1852 is our diplomatic instructor this day. He asserted a policy upon which we will stand and defy interference; he touched chords of country which will vibrate while this war shall last; he lifted the clear signal to nations which may in some day of the future become the flaming cross of deliverance to Mexico. In the ripeness of his age he was, at the hour of his death, I apprehend, one of the most just and equitable and learned and best balanced expounders of international law on the globe. If he might have lived to execute his purpose, the volume which he proposed upon the laws and rights of nations would, I believe, have placed him at the head of that sublime jurisprudence which is founded upon the historic lessons of Christian civilization.

We are about to bury our foremost scholar and orator. Do not suppose that I intend to analyze now the remarkable eloquence of Mr. Everett. I only allude to it. He was a perfect literary artist; but this idea of him has in some minds been the source of most unjust conception as to the wider domain of his force and his power. And this injustice, while it is according to experience, is also unphilosophical. Mr. Webster in his practice was scarcely less observant of the dramatic circumstances of public eloquence; but rising on broader and deeper foundations, being less frequent and conversant with the schools, cast in the mould of country life and more familiar with its sympathies, and more than all, trained in that most democratical discipline of trials before juries, he escaped the reputation of speaking according to art. No man, however, ever understood this art better than he. With him, this characteristic assumed the form not of a fine art, but of the power of drama.

It is not worth while to cite illustrations, but the fact is known to all close critics. His library, his study was veiled to the world, but he himself passed the long and solemn hours behind the curtain, before his stately form emerged to attract the wonder of men. Mr. Everett never could extinguish the midnight lamp, never could disguise the alcoves he loved. But no man in our day has painted so well, and left no specific trace of how the colors had been applied. I doubt if at any time, until within the last ten years, educated men have quite done him justice in this particular. Art is apt to conceal the substance of greatness; manner oftentimes overshades the matter. It is so through all of life. Robert Walpole was really one of the ablest of British premiers; but his adherence to the arts of his office lost him the credit of his administration in the popular judgment. He who shall pronounce your formal eulogy upon Mr. Everett cannot say that his eloquence had exactly the sweeping majesty which bore Chatham or Webster through periods swelling and resounding like a national anthem, or like the thunders of great armadas on the sea; such passages come rarely to human ears; they

> "Come as the winds come, when forests are rended :
> Come as the waves come, when navies are stranded."

But he shall accord to him the finest and most complete proportions that have marked any orator of this age. The mould of personal form, all the graces, the voice, the cadences, partly constitutional and partly acquired, all that is histrionic and attractive, all that nature could furnish and art could add, belonged in largest measure and in purest style to him. But this is only the form, the style and the stage. There was a greatness of character behind all this. You sometimes overlooked the depth of his philosophy, the richness of his reflection, only because he pleased and beguiled you. Not a sentence unnecessary, not a word unessential, can you find in all that he has said or written. He never rejected truisms if they might be profitable; but he illuminated them with the choicest colors of the rainbow. He never neglected the lessons of religion, or science, or experience, but he had the genius to make them winning as a first love. He had exquisite humor and subtle art; but if it escaped his tongue or pen it was quite likely to mingle with some pensive thought that toned it down to marvellous sobriety and beauty. His smile on the platform was of that kind which we are told belongs to genius, because melancholy is a part of genius; and yet it pleased us, because it was uncommon and serene. He had a peculiar tenderness of oratory.

But the eloquence of Mr. Everett ended not here. He had all knowledge, all gifts, all tongues. No man of this generation, save Macaulay, had equal command of the treasures of the ages. No orator in America, from the first until now, has so woven into his addresses the instructions of history. This I have thought to be his specialty. His memory was comprehensive, retentive, and perfect. He had read everything, and he remembered all that he had read. There is no such treasury for an orator as that, if he have all the other plenitudes, powers and graces, as Mr. Everett possessed them. Accordingly, for an entire generation, he has instructed his country in historical knowledge and historical analogies, and his instructions have had the charm of freshness, and naturalness, and fitness. In this department of usefulness, broad enough for the highest ambition, he has had no equal among all his countrymen. In this we have always delighted to call him our master and our guide. And thus, to our Congress and our Cabinets, to our cultured men and to all our people, he has been a splendid educator. His instructions have descended from his own elevated table-land, through our social strata, purifying and ennobling every class of mind, fascinating by their gorgeous but natural array, and carrying on their wing the transport of communicated thought and knowledge. I appropriate to him the eulogy from Milton; "I shall detain you no longer in the demonstration, but strait conduct ye to a hill-side, were I will point ye out the right path of a virtuous and noble education; laborious indeed at the first ascent, but also so smooth, so green, so full of goodly prospect, and melodious sounds on every side, that the harp of Orpheus was not more charming."

His greatest days were his last. The country did not know him perfectly until 1861. Then he renewed his youth ; then he broke away from his own traditions and associations, and mounted to that wise, large patriotism which has guided twenty loyal millions to life and glory. He waited not for others, nor for the victory of our arms; but in those first days of war and gloom, his voice sounded like a clarion over this land. Almighty God be praised that he has been spared to us these four years! In these temples of your eloquence, in that commercial metropolis where his counsel was more needed, everywhere, and every day, by public speech and through the popular press, he has confirmed hesitating men at home, he has inspired your armies in the field. These victories which fill the air to-day, peal grandly over his inanimate form ; they cannot wake him from sleep, but they are a fitting salute for his burial. He passes to his rest when the whole heaven is lighted up to proclaim that his mission has been accomplished. The same page of the calendar shall repeat to the next age, THE DEATH OF EVERETT AND THE NEW LIFE OF HIS COUNTRY.

Mr. James M. Beebe offered the following additional resolution, which was inserted in the list originally reported, and the whole series was then unanimously adopted : —

Resolved, That as a tribute of respect to the memory of Mr. Everett, this meeting recommend to our fellow-citizens that the banks, insurances offices, and other places of business be closed to-morrow at the hour set apart for his funeral.

In accordance with one of the resolutions the Chairman appointed the following-named gentlemen a Committee to take measures for the erection of a statue in honor of Edward Everett.

Charles G. Loring,
Robert C. Winthrop,
George Livermore,
J. H. Wolcott,
Geo. B. Upton,
Geo. C. Richardson,
Otis Norcross,
Edward S. Tobey,
Nathaniel Thayer,
Jas. M. Beebe,
James Lawrence,
Eben Dale,
Martin Brimmer,
F. E. Parker,
Gardner Brewer,
Sidney Bartlett,
Geo. S. Hillard,
Daniel N. Haskell,
Charles F. Dunbar,
Geo. Wm. Bond,
J. Tisdale Bradlee,
John S. Tyler,
Wm. Endicott, jr.
Henry A. Pierce,
J. W. Seaver,
Henry P. Kidder,
Wm. B. Fowle, jr.

Geo. Ticknor,
Jacob Bigelow,
J. Mason Warren,
Wm. Amory,
Chas. Amory,
Edw. Austin,
J. J. Dixwell,
Sam'l D. Crane,
W. W. Clapp, jr.
Josiah Quincy,
Oliver Ditson,
Jos. T. Bailey,
J. G. Palfrey,
Geo. W. Messinger,
S. K. Lothrop,
C. G. Greene,
Albert Fearing,
Sam'l H. Walley,
Rufus Ellis,
J. Ingersoll Bowditch,
Chas. O. Rogers,
Francis Bacon,
Wm. Gray,
Henry I. Bowditch,
Albert Bowker,
Albert J. Wright,
O. W. Holmes,

Samuel G. Ward,	Thomas G. Appleton,
Richard H. Dana,	James L. Little,
Thomas Gaffield,	Peter Harvey,

J. M. Wightman.

On motion, the name of His Honor Mayor Lincoln was added to the Committee.

The meeting then dissolved.

FUNERAL.

THE FUNERAL.

THE funeral of Mr. Everett took place on Thursday, January 19. The public solemnities were under the charge of the Committee of the City Council, and were conducted with as little display as the proprieties of the occasion would permit. Since the death of Mr. Webster no such general and profound manifestations of sorrow had been exhibited. The announcement made by order of the President of the United States, on Sunday, had led many to expect that he would honor the obsequies with his presence; his official duties, however, rendered it impracticable; and on Wednesday, a despatch was received from Mr. Seward, stating that fact, and tendering to the Commonwealth the condolence of the President and the Heads of Departments, " on the lamented death of Edward Everett, who was worthy to be enrolled among the noblest of the nation's benefactors."

The public services were held in the First Church in Chauncy Street, where Mr. Everett had been a constant attendant for many years. Although the weather was unusually cold, and the ground was covered with snow, the streets in the vicinity, and along the whole route of the procession, were crowded with people long before the hour appointed for the ceremonies to begin. It being understood that the galleries of the church would be reserved for ladies, an immense number congregated in front of the doors as early as ten o'clock, and waited patiently, until the doors were opened at eleven o'clock. All public buildings, and many of the places of business in the city were closed. In the Merchants' Exchange, the Public Library, the Mercantile Library, and the Union Club House, emblems of mourning were displayed, and on public and private buildings the national flag appeared at half-mast.

Previous to the public ceremonies in the church, there were private services at Mr. Everett's house in Summer Street, at which Rev. Edward Everett Hale officiated. None but the relatives and intimate personal friends of the deceased were present. The Independent Corps of Cadets, Lieutenant-Colonel Holmes, performed guard duty in front of the house during the services, and at their conclusion escorted the remains to the church. The following-named gentlemen acted as pallbearers : —

EMORY WASHBURN,
Ex-Governor of Massachusetts.

F. W. LINCOLN, JR.
Mayor of the City.

THOMAS HILL,
President of Harvard University.

GEORGE T. BIGELOW,
Chief Justice Supreme Court.

GEORGE TICKNOR,
Trustee Public Library.

ROBERT C. WINTHROP,
President Historical Society.

CHARLES G. LORING,
Vice-President Union Club.

ASA GRAY,
Pres. of Acad. of Arts and Sciences.

J. D. GRAHAM,
Colonel United States Army.

SILAS H. STRINGHAM,
Rear-Admiral United States Navy.

In accordance with the notice issued by the Chief Marshal, the delegations from various organizations which had signified their desire to participate in the ceremonies, assembled at the City Hall at half-past eleven o'clock, and marched thence, at twelve o'clock, to the church. His Excellency the Governor, the members of his staff, the President of the State Senate, the Speaker of the House, the Joint Committee from the General Court, and the Overseers of Harvard University, arrived at the church at the same time.

Shortly after twelve o'clock, the body was borne into the church, and up the main aisle. The entire congregation arose and remained standing, until the coffin was placed upon the table below the pulpit. A chant was performed by the choir; and Rev. James Walker, D. D., the venerable ex-President of Harvard University, then offered prayer, and read appropriate selections from the Scriptures. Rev. Rufus Ellis, pastor of the church, made the following address —

We are on our way to commit to the earth all that was mortal of a great and good, and justly famous man; a man so great, so good, so famous, that the honors decreed for him by the head of the nation will be most gratefully rendered, and that to the very letter of the decree, at home and abroad, wherever the national name and authority are recognized. We have paused for a few moments and laid down our burden within these consecrated walls — so familiar and dear to him who has gone from us — that we may acknowledge the Giver of Life, the Father of Him who is the resurrection and the life, the best and the only comforter. It is for this that we are here, believing that our burden will be lightened for hands, which are so ready to hang down, if only we can obtain help from God.

And yet, before we seek the refuge of prayer, in the name and the faith of Christ, a word must be

10

spoken to this great company — a word from heart to heart — of him whom you revered and admired, and loved; for I am sure that the most halting speech, so it be sincere, will do more justice than silence, to the spirit of this hour, so solemn, and yet so rich in memories and in hopes. In these few and swiftly passing moments, I cannot tell the story of this grandly completed life, as full of works as of days, from its boyhood, mature as manhood, to its age, vigorous as youth. I may not attempt any analysis of this fine intellect, or try to explore with you, the hiding-places of this great power. I shall undertake no delineation of a character which was always most admired by those who were brought nearest to it, and which like some of the works of the most conscientious artists, was most finished where it made the least show. We are on our way to a grave, and our words must be few, and they may be very simple, for uppermost in our minds and abounding in our hearts, are proud and grateful thoughts of the departed, which the tongue of the most unlettered might tell.

What is it, friends, that has made this man so very dear to the people, I do not say to scholars, to the few, but to the people, yea, their foremost citizen in these times when God has made "a man more precious than fine gold, even a man than the golden wedge of Ophir!" Why is the announcement of his sudden death, by the President of the United States, only the utterance of a nation's sorrowing heart? I answer, — you answer, — not merely because he was your scholar

and a ripe and good one; not merely because he was
your orátor, one of the most eloquent and instructive
of men, your chief speaker for every grand and good
occasion; not merely because of his life-long service
to letters and to the education of the people; not
merely because of his labors for the State, at home
and abroad, in ordinary times, honorable, admirable, as
he ever was in these things; but because in the hour
of sore trial, and when the nation's very life hung in
the balance, and patriotism was something more than
an idle word for the trifler to ring changes upon, he
has proved himself to be first, last, only, and altogether
a Christian patriot, an American, indeed, in whom was
no guile, resolved at all costs to himself, of old friendships if need be, of old prejudices, our costliest
possessions, to do his whole duty to the land and the
people of his affections, as to the mother that bore him
and nourished him, and led him up to his grand and
serviceable manhood. I mean no disparagement of
former services; nay; where some might criticise, I
should justify, and yet on this day of his solemn
burial I say honor to this large, this regal soul, which
could not sacrifice itself to obsolete ideas, or go about,
with the dead burying their dead, or crush the
throbbing life of to-day under any old traditions;
honor to him who could see that old principles may
demand new methods, and that the wisdom of yesterday may be the folly of to-day. During these grand
historic years, years in which many an hour has been
worth whole months of commonplace existence, with

the rest of the nation, he has been passing through the refiner's fire, and you have found, dear friends, to your joy, for nothing refreshes and delights us so much as to be able to reverence and admire, and love — you have found that the finest gold was in him, that he was more than your great scholar, more than your great orator, more than your trusted statesman and diplomatist, that he was your great citizen and your brother man, your country his country, your political faith his political faith — not a man to babble garrulously of foreign despotisms, but a lover and a servant of our republican institutions, his heart throbbing with your hearts, and alive with sacred national memories, and precious hopes for humanity sighing to be uplifted and redeemed. How manly, how consistent, how steadfast, how unwearied he has been, in all his glorious speaking and doing from the first moment when our nation's life was assailed, to that day so fatal to us, but so honorable to him, when weighed down as he was by sickness, and already entering into the death-shadow, he asked help in such eloquent words for those who, as we hope, are ceasing to be our enemies, in the name of that holy and sweet charity which St. Paul, inspired by our Lord, has taught us, saying, "If thine enemy hunger, feed him." So he took up in the time of his age and for his last public act, the sacred office which he had laid down in youth, and was found at the last a gospel preacher.

When the history of our nation's regeneration shall be written, — and it will be an illuminated record, —

when victory and peace, which are as sure to be ours as that the sun burns in the heavens, shall be the reward of patient struggle, no name shall shine out more brightly upon the page, or be pronounced more thankfully by the lips, than the name of him for whom we both rejoice and mourn to-day. In these last great years we have seen the beauty, we have breathed in the fragrance of the fair, consummate flower of a noble plant. Never has the bright sun of his life shone with such refulgent brightness as when it neared the setting, but was even more a giant than when it climbed the morning sky. And all this strength was blended with so much gentleness, all this earnest speech was so free from bitterness and wrath, all this public virtue was bound up with so much private worth and household love and Christian faith. Alas! that his day must needs come! Strange! that when so many only cumber the earth, and eat and drink, but do *not* die to-morrow! Alas! that we are here and without him, with only this sacred dust, precious indeed in our sight and to be borne away most tenderly, and yet so sadly reminding us, that himself is gone. Alas! for our necessity is still so great and our counsellor was so wise and so noble, so prudent and so charitable, so thoroughly furnished for the hour! Would, we say, that God who hath an eternity to give from, had given more time to him who knew so well how to redeem time! And yet, my friends, who are we that we should reply against God? and hath the Christ been so long time with us and have we not yet learned to trust utterly in the

Divine Providence, in Him that taketh away as well as in Him that giveth, in Him who said by the lips of his own dear Son, "Except a corn of wheat fall into the ground and die, it abideth alone, but if it die, it bringeth forth much fruit?" Let us rather give thanks for the life in the light of which we have lived and which God hath crowned with glory and honor and immortality, for its years of devotion to the things which are highest and holiest; stricken, bereaved, let us bow reverently and submissively to the Divine decree, and have no will but that Will which is forever Love; let us have faith that with his blessing who appoints for us our works and our days, and meteth out our span with an unerring wisdom, there shall come forth, life from this death, beauty from these ashes, life and beauty for earth as well as for heaven. Being dead he doth yet speak to us, if only we have open ears, more eloquently than even he, worthy to be named with the most famous masters of speech since the world began, could speak to us, being yet alive. But why do I say "being dead," seeing that the righteous live forevermore, seeing that their reward is with the Lord and the care of them with the most High, and that below and above, He giveth to them a beautiful kingdom and a glorious crown and an abiding ministry? Honor to the dead! and what fitter honor can we pay to the dead than by consecrating ourselves, about these remains, to that dear country whose holy cause he who is gone can plead no longer in the name of Humanity, of Christ, of God, to whom in death, and in life be glory forever and ever! Amen.

Rev. Mr. Ellis, then offered prayer, and after a hymn had been sung, he descended from the pulpit and read a portion of the burial service. An anthem was sung, and the services were concluded with a benediction, pronounced by Rev. Dr. Walker.

The funeral procession was formed soon after one o'clock, under the direction of the following officers : —

Chief Marshal.

BREVET BRIG. GEN. F. A. OSBORN.

Aids.

GEO. H. KINGSBURY,   LIEUT.-COL. O. W PEABODY.

Marshals.

DAVID H. COOLIDGE,	A. J. C. SOWDON,
T. B. WINCHESTER,	S. A. STETSON,
ELIAS B. GLEASON,	CAPT. J. C. MAKER,
MAJ. EDW. C. RICHARDSON,	W. RALPH EMERSON,
H. H. COOLIDGE,	E. R. MEARS,
CAPT. J. H. LOMBARD.	CAPT. JOHN N. PARTRIDGE.

The military escort was under the command of Lieutenant-Colonel C. C. Holmes, with Lieut. G. C. Winsor acting as Aid-de-Camp.

The order of the procession was as follows : —

Drum Corps.
First Unattached Co. Infantry, M. V. M. (Lincoln Guard,)
Capt. M. E. Bigelow.
Marine Band.
Battalion of Four Companies U. S. Marines.   Capt. Lowry,
Commanding.

Chelsea Band, (mounted.)

Company B, First Battalion Light Dragoons, (Boston Light Dragoons,) Capt. Charles T. Stevens.

Company A, First Battalion Light Dragoons, (National Lancers,) Capt. Lucius Slade.

Pall Bearers in Carriages.

Brigade Band.

Independent Corps of Cadets, Major Charles B. Raymond, Commanding.

Cadets.   HEARSE   Cadets.

Howitzer Battery of the Cadets.

Relatives of the Deceased in Carriages.

Chief Marshal and Aids.

City Council, School Committee, and Trustees of the Public Library of the City of Boston.

His Excellency, the Governor, and his Staff.

Executive and Legislative Departments of the Commonwealth.

Corporation and Overseers of Harvard College.

Officers of the Army and Navy.

Justices of the Supreme Judicial Court.

Delegations from : —

American Antiquarian Society.

Massachusetts Historical Society.

Massachusetts Charitable Mechanic Association.

Boston Board of Trade.

Professors and Students of Harvard College.

City Government of Worcester.

City Government of Charlestown.

Bunker Hill Monument Association.

Lexington Monument Association.

New England Historic Genealogical Society.

Franklin Medal Scholars.
Mercantile Library Association.
Committee, Master, and Pupils of the Everett School.
Ancient and Honorable Artillery Company, in citizens' dress.

The procession began to move at two o'clock over the following route: through Chauncy, Washington, School, Beacon, Charles, and Cambridge streets to Cambridge Bridge. The bells on all the churches in the city were tolled, and minute-guns were fired by a section of Light Artillery, on the Common, during the passage of the procession through the city. The streets were lined with spectators, many of whom reverently uncovered their heads as the hearse passed. At Cambridge Bridge a portion of the procession was dismissed. The Cadets and the Brigade Band, were conveyed to Harvard Square in cars. The procession was there reformed again, and then proceeded to Mount Auburn Cemetery. The remains of Mr. Everett were interred in the family lot, No. 17 Magnolia Avenue. There were no services at this place. Wreaths of white flowers and evergreens were placed upon the coffin, and as it was lowered into the grave, the Brigade Band began the solemn strains of the "Dead March" in *Saul*.

11

PROCEEDINGS OF THE SCHOOL COMMITTEE.

IN THE SCHOOL COMMITTEE.

AT a meeting of the School Committee of the City of Boston, on Tuesday, January 24, 1865, His Honor the Mayor in the Chair, Rev. S. K. Lothrop, D. D., made the following remarks : —

MR. PRESIDENT: Since the last meeting of this Board, an event has occurred which has thrown a gloom over our city, our community, our country. Edward Everett, whose name for more than fifty years has been held in honor among us, associated with learning, literature, eloquence, statesmanship, philanthropy, and patriotism, — who has filled a great variety of public offices and adorned them all by rare abilities and eminent fidelity, — whose career has been marked by an unspotted integrity, purity, and a large usefulness, has suddenly been called from among us, and the places that have so long known him here, shall know him no more forever. The City Government have taken appropriate notice of this sad event. The authorities of the State have not let it pass unobserved ; the Chief Magistrate of the nation has called the attention of the country to the loss of a devoted patriot — its foremost private citizen, — and as the intelligence of this event is borne over the land and over the sea, many in all parts of the Christian world, will receive it with a deep regret, and give it some form of reverent notice. A medal scholar of the Boston Public Schools, receiving the first rudiments of his education at those institutions which are under the special charge of this Board; retaining at all times and up to the close of his life a strong interest, not only in the great cause of popular education, but especially in the Public Schools of our city, it is due not only to him, but to ourselves, that our Records should contain some expression of our gratitude for his services, our sorrow at his death, our respect for his memory.

I ask leave, therefore, Mr. President, to submit the following resolutions, and, if adopted, to have them placed upon our Records : —

Whereas, The Hon. Edward Everett died suddenly, after a brief illness, at his residence in Summer Street, on Sunday morning, the 15th instant, the School Committee of the City of Boston, on this their first meeting after his decease, desire to adopt, and place upon their Records the following resolutions.

Resolved, That we share in the universal regret and sorrow which this event awakens, and sympathize in all the private and public tokens of profound respect so justly paid to the memory of one who has enriched our literature by his learning and scholarship, illustrated our history, and instructed our people, by many eloquent orations and addresses, elevated public and political life among us by faithful service in exalted station, and by the dignity, purity, and unstained integrity of his character and conduct; who has often stirred our patriotism by his fervent appeals, confirmed it by his cogent arguments, guided by his illustrious example, and who, through a long life of unremitted industry, and the noble exercise of great and versatile powers in manifold positions and offices, and by a beautiful exhibition of the Christian virtues, in private and domestic relations, has adorned our common humanity, and left us, in his fame, a legacy to be cherished with gratitude and pride.

Resolved, That it is specially incumbent upon this Board, instituted for the promotion, and entrusted with the guardianship of the Public Schools of the city, to recognize and honor his name and services as connected with the cause of popular education. Receiving his own first distinction in life — the Franklin Medal — twice, first at the North School in 1804, and again at our Public Latin School in 1806, he has never ceased, for half a century, amid all his honors and avocations, to feel a deep interest in these primary fountains of learning, whose healing waters are for the enlightenment of the whole people; and has repeatedly manifested his respect and confidence by using them for the education of his children and his children's children; and his Chief Magistracy of our Commonwealth, wise and firm in its administration of all our affairs, was distinguished by two events, — the inauguration of the Board of Education, and of our State Normal Schools, which are as honorable testimonials of patriotic wisdom and usefulness as any incumbent has ever left in the Chair of State, and grandly beneficent in the effect they have had to enlarge, elevate, and advance that popular education which is the secret of the past and present position, power, and prosperity of Massachusetts.

Resolved, That, while we bow in devout submission to the Divine Will, which has removed from among us so eminent and useful a citizen, it is alike a duty, a pleasure, and a benefit to recall with gratitude his distinguished services, to cherish the memory of all that was beautiful, useful, honorable, and Christian in his life and character, and make it an incentive in our individual hearts to a like fidelity, — a fidelity that in us, also, shall meet the measure of our ability and our opportunities.

The Resolutions were unanimously adopted.

PROCEEDINGS OF THE TRUSTEES OF THE PUBLIC LIBRARY.

12

TRUSTEES OF THE PUBLIC LIBRARY.

A special meeting of the Trustees of the Public Library was held on the 17th of Jan. 1865, at 11 o'clock, A. M., to take suitable notice of the death of their President, the Hon. Edward Everett. The following resolutions were offered by George Ticknor, Esq., chairman of the meeting, and were unanimously adopted by the Board : —

Resolved, That, while the Trustees of the Public Library, in common with all their fellow-citizens, look back, with proud gratitude, to the record of the eminent services rendered by Mr. Everett in trusts and ways so various and so distinct, not only to the highest interests of our country and our Commonwealth, but to the interests of letters and religion, and to the promotion of all that is good, faithful, and worthy everywhere, during his long life, an uncommon portion of which has been marked and honored on both sides of the Atlantic,— we yet feel at this sad moment an obligation more especially resting on this Board thankfully to acknowledge, how much is due to him from our own city as one of those,

who earliest and most earnestly, counselled and promoted
the foundation of this *Public Library*, to whose interests
and progress,— amidst the many high and graver claims
that were constantly crowded on his care,— he devoted
himself faithfully from its first beginnings down to the
very day before his death, acting, during the whole of its
organized existence, with uniform wisdom, gentleness,
and dignity, as its presiding officer.

Resolved, That, as a mark of respect to the memory of
our late honored and lamented President, and, in deference
to the feeling of this whole community, the Trustees direct
the Library to be closed during the day of his interment,
and that it be draped in mourning for the thirty days subsequent.

Resolved, That the chairman of this meeting address to
the family of Mr. Everett a certified copy of these proceedings, expressing to them, at the same time, our heartfelt sympathy in this, their great sorrow, and commending
them to the gracious God in whom he always trusted, and
to the Christian consolations, in which — during such
times of trial and bereavement as come to all men — he
found an unfailing support.

PROCEEDINGS OF THE MASSACHUSETTS LEGISLATURE.

MASSACHUSETTS LEGISLATURE.

IN THE SENATE.

MONDAY, JAN. 16, 1865.

Mr. Wentworth, of Middlesex, offered the following order: —

Whereas, intelligence has been received announcing the death of the Hon. Edward Everett, at his residence in this city,

Ordered, That a committee of five on the part of the Senate, with such as the House may join, be appointed to consider and report what measures it may be proper for the Legislature to adopt as a testimonial of its gratitude for the public services and respect for the memory of the illustrious dead.

The order was adopted, and Senators Wentworth of Middlesex, Loud of Plymouth, Parker of Suffolk, Foster of Essex, and Kneil of Hampden were appointed as the Committee on the part of the Senate.

IN THE HOUSE.

The order from the Senate in regard to measures to be taken in relation to the decease of the Hon. Edward Everett was concurred in and the following gentlemen were joined to the Senate committee on the subject: Messrs. Kimball of Boston, Wells of Chicopee, Scudder of Dorchester, Stone of Charlestown, Hills of Boston, Stone of Waltham, Gallup of Brookfield, Dwelley of Hanover Warren of Windsor, and Hall of Dennis.

Mr. KIMBALL, of Boston, moved that, out of respect for the memory of Mr. Everett, the House immediately adjourn.

Adjourned.

IN THE SENATE.

THURSDAY, JANUARY 20, 1865.

A communication was received from His Excellency the Governor, as follows: —

HON. J. E. FIELD, *President of the Senate:* —

SIR: I perceive that the Senate will be in session at 10 o'clock this morning to consider and adopt appropriate measures in honor of the memory of our late illustrious fellow-citizen, EDWARD EVERETT.

In the utmost sympathy with the Senate, and sharing its sense of bereavement, the Executive Department of the Commonwealth will cordially unite with the General Court in every demonstration of affectionate respect for the departed which it may adopt. The Governor and Council propose to attend the funeral to-day in a body. The military staff of the Commonwealth Headquarters have been directed to report at the Council Chamber at 11 o'clock A. M., and an appropriate military detachment is under orders to perform the duty of escorting the funeral procession, the Independent Corps of Cadets acting as a guard of honor to the remains of the deceased statesman, whose body guard they were in his former capacity of Governor of Massachusetts.

I am, sir, with high respect, your obedient and humble servant,

JOHN A. ANDREW.

Mr. Wentworth of Middlesex, from the committee on resolutions of respect to the memory of Mr. Everett, submitted the following, which were read by the Clerk: —

Resolved. That, as members of the Senate and House of Representatives of the Commonwealth of Massachusetts, we deem it our public duty to express the profound emotions with which we, and the people whom we represent, have received the intelligence of the death of the Hon. Edward Everett.

Resolved. That we mourn with deep regret the loss of a citizen who, for fifty years, has been the pride and ornament of the Commonwealth; who in early youth attracted public attention as a poet and scholar, and during a period in which he was the active associate of three generations of men had never ceased to occupy it as an accomplished man of letters and a finished and captivating orator; who united to singular gifts of speech and action an equally unusual power of application and habit of industry; who touched no subject, however light, without leaving upon it the mark of conscientious care, and who investigated no question, however grave, without throwing over it the inimitable charm of genius;

who, having begun active life with the patience and ripeness of age, still retained in age the grace and spirit of youth, and, when he had passed the allotted age of man, so completely filled the public eye and satisfied the public expectation, that had he no better claim for gratitude, his death would still be an irreparable loss.

Resolved. That we recollect with pride that the life of Mr. Everett was spent in the public service, and that we cherish in respectful remembrance the fidelity and signal success with which he filled the highest offices of his native State; that he administered these great public trusts as a personal duty, and devoted to all their details the same attention which he bestowed on his most splendid efforts; that he added dignity to the national councils by his profound learning as a statesman, and maintained the national honor abroad by the intelligence and wisdom of his diplomacy; that he was never seduced by public indulgence to act on any measure without thorough investigation, and during his long and eventful public service, never failed to appreciate the magnitude and difficulty of the questions before him, and to give to them, all the strength of his great talents, and the illumination of his various knowledge. Nor are we to forget that he dignified his public station by private virtues; by the profession of a Christian faith, and the practice of a Christian life.

Resolved. That, while we thus gratefully recognize the eminent usefulness and importance of Mr. Everett's public life, we regard, and would here commemorate, as his highest title to honor and gratitude from the people of this Commonwealth, the timely and decisive service which he has rendered during the last four years to our common country, in her struggle for national unity and national existence ; and that we consider the promptness with which he embraced the cause of the Union, the distinctness with which he saw the vital issues of the present war, the cordial support which he gave to the Government, the research and unequalled clearness of the productions by which he sought to form, and did form, an enlightened public opinion, the temperate and luminous papers by which he upheld our cause to the world, the confidence which his presence and his speech inspired in the success of our arms, and, more than all, the ardent love of country which animated his spoken and written words, and prompted him to those grand enterprises of national charity, of which he has left so little for others to complete, as the crowning glory of his long and brilliant life, and as entitling him to an imperishable place in the history of the United States as an ILLUSTRIOUS CITIZEN.

Resolved. That an eulogy on his life and character, be pronounced before the Executive and Legislative branches of the government of the Commonwealth, at some time during the present session.

Resolved. That His Excellency the Governor be requested to transmit a copy of these resolves to the family of Mr. Everett.

Resolved. That a Committee, consisting of the President and ten members on the part of the Senate, and the Speaker and twenty members on the part of the House, be appointed to attend the funeral of the deceased.

Mr. Wentworth addressed the Senate as follows : —

The resolutions which have been read to the Senate are designed to express the sentiments of the Legislature upon the melancholy event they are intended to commemorate. It is peculiarly fitting that we should, in an appropriate manner, and by public action, call the attention of our fellow-citizens to the loss the country has sustained in the death of Edward Everett. The orator, the statesman, the patriot, the philanthropist and Christian, is no more! For forty years, with few and short intermissions, the exertions of Mr. Everett have been devoted to the public in various positions in the service of this, his native State, and of the nation.

Of the eminent ability and success which has marked his entire public career, of the patriotic efforts which have so signally illustrated the last years of his valuable life, and of the philanthropic labors which have been so gracefully and bounteously yielded by him to every call of suffering and distress, there will be fitting occasion elsewhere for others to speak, — an occasion when a delineation of his character, life, and services will give to mankind a splendid example of the highest talent employed for the noblest ends ; of a life devoted with unusual fidelity to the welfare of the human race, and which has adorned the policy, the politics, and the literature of his country. I content myself with expressing my entire concurrence with the Legislative action proposed, and move the adoption of the resolutions.

Mr. WORCESTER of Essex said: —

MR. PRESIDENT: I find myself constrained to violate a resolution which I had formed, in coming into this body, — that I would not occupy the attention of the Senate, except for a few moments at a time, — perhaps, for months to come. But I owe a debt of gratitude to Mr. Everett, and must speak of him somewhat with the feelings of a son. Were it not for this, my voice would probably now be silent.

It was my privilege to be a member of the College at Cambridge, when he returned from his four years of sojourn in Europe, to enter upon his duties as Eliot Professor of Greek literature. I may almost say, that his lecture-room in the old Harvard Hall was the birthplace of my mind. Sure I am, that no one of all the officers of the College had such an awakening power of influence upon my own mind; and what is true of myself, I believe, was also true of my class generally. We were one of the five classes only, if I remember rightly, that enjoyed his instructions, in the senior year.

He laid out a programme for a course of lectures upon Greek literature and the antiquities of the classic lands, which, instead of some twenty-five or thirty lectures, would have required three hundred for its entire completion. His manner of lecturing was colloquial and exceedingly familiar. He would read a few pages from his carefully prepared manuscripts, and then turn from the written lecture, and indulge himself in extemporized *excurses*, suggested by some word or association. In these he was no less interesting and instructive, than in the most finished parts of his lectures, as he read them in his deliberate and earnest manner. Often have I seen him roll up his papers, and close the hour, when he did not appear to have delivered more than a third, if more than a sixth part, of what he had written for the occasion.

It seemed to be his constant aim to arouse the interest and the emulation of the students, in exertions to qualify themselves for distinguished usefulness. He has been represented as if he was not a man of warm heart, but was characteristically cold and unapproachable. He certainly was not thus, as he appeared in the lecture-room, and as I saw him at other times, when he gave a few of us private instructions in an extra course of study, to which all were kindly invited.

He seemed as if he wished to break down those conventional barriers, which were designed probably to keep the students at a respectful, but which practically kept them at a *disrespectful*, distance from the officers. And it is no disparagement to any of those with whom he was associated in the instruction of the College, to say that no one of them was more highly esteemed. He was truly beloved.

It was most easy to follow him as he lectured. A second or third rate reporter could have taken down almost every word, whether he was reading or extemporizing. I took myself extended notes of his lectures. And as I yesterday looked over some eighty or a hundred pages, I was surprised on being reminded of the great amount of labor which he accomplished, and the range of topics which he illustrated, or alluded to, as worthy of remembrance or research.

The first time I saw Mr. Everett, was in the latter part of my freshman year, — the summer of 1819, — and when he had just returned from Europe. His appearance then, when but twenty-five years of age, was not in the full and somewhat portly, bodily form which we have seen in his later years. His countenance was that of a hard student, and his bearing was by no means that of a man who gave promise of the length of days which he has been permitted to enjoy. It was a slender and diminutive figure, even, which he presented, when he walked from University Hall across the College yard, as I have seen him, — leaning upon the arm of his younger brother John, who, as he now comes before my memory in his stalwart form, " from his shoulders and upward was higher." Some have thought, that in native intellectual endowment, that brother, who went down to an early grave, had as much superiority, as he had in bodily presence, over the lamented man whose death we are now called to mourn.

From the reputation which preceded Mr. Everett's coming to enter upon his duties as Professor, the students had high expectations. The first displays which he made before us, were from the pulpit. But although he drew large audiences, and was highly extolled and glorified by many, I do not think that he made any great impression upon the under-graduates. The pulpit was not his appropriate place. I heartily rejoiced when he withdrew from it, and gave himself so devotedly to the instruction of the College classes ; and afterwards to the instruction of the country and of the world.

Soon after his return from Europe, he was editor of the *North American Review*, which he *renewed*, by giving it a character and reputation such as it never had before. The students were much interested in the articles which he wrote for it, and which they thought could be easily identified. The style of those articles had a great effect, in stimulating them to cultivate a high order of literary composition. We were specially interested in the articles, which vindicated our institutions and character against the mendacious reports of British travellers in America, and the savage assaults of the Edinburgh and London Quarterly Reviews. At this time there was much written in the spirit of Sydney Smith's sneering interrogatory, — "*Who reads an American book?*"

In refuting the statements and repelling the assaults of British travellers and reviewers, Mr. Everett came forth with a *manliness* which he had not before displayed. His compositions had often seemed to belong rather to the feminine than to the masculine gender. While he showed that he had the same delicacy of taste and kindliness of temper, which had been so admirably exhibited by Washington Irving, in the essays of the *Sketch Book*, which portrayed and defended our national character, — he also showed a vigor and masterly strength, which, perhaps, he owed in part at least, to his intimacy with Webster, whom he so greatly admired, and with whom he so intensely sympathized. In those vindications of our country which appeared in the *North American*, from the pen of Mr. Everett, you may see the germs or the elements of the same patriotism which has so nobly distinguished the efforts of these last years of his life.

He could say very hard things in very mild words. He could take a man's head off, by a feather, as well as by any more potent instrument. An example of his manner now occurs to me. He was commenting upon some flagrant statements. " This," said he, " is a species of fiction in which gentlemen of veracity are not accustomed to indulge."

One or two articles he wrote on the Missouri question, with signal ability. One of these, I think was in the early part of 1820, when he reviewed the history of slavery in our country, — referring to the principles and sentiments of the founders of the republic, and earnestly imploring, that the area of the " peculiar institution" should be no farther extended. These views he seems to have modified, after he became a member of Congress: perhaps more *seemingly*, than in reality, yet affording too much occasion for the terrible rebuke of John Randolph, who, as some will remember, gave him to understand, that slave-holder as he was himself, he had little respect for the heart or the head of any man, from

14

the North, who would stand up there to apologize for Southern slavery.

In August, 1824, Mr. Everett delivered an oration before the Phi Beta Kappa Society, which was received with the highest applause. General Lafayette had just arrived, on a visit to the United States, and his coming stirred up and called forth all the patriotic feeling, which could be moved by the remembrances and associations of the revolutionary war. His presence in the assembly at Cambridge added greatly to the interest of that 27th day of August, — a day most memorable in Mr. Everett's public life.

The subject of the oration, as then stated by the orator, was " The peculiar motives to intellectual exertion in America." In a revised edition of Mr. Everett's works, the oration appears under the title of " Circumstances favorable to the progress of literature in the United States." In the treatment of this subject, he displayed a wealth of learning and a wealth of language, which perfectly amazed his auditory, and far exceeded all the most sanguine expectations of his greatest admirers. It would be utterly impossible to describe the effect produced as with his graphic and thrilling power, as from an inspiration he depicted, " the theatre upon which the intellect of America was to appear;" " the motives to its exertion;" " the mass to be influenced by its efforts;" " the crowd to witness its energies;" and "the glory to crown its success." And when in his peroration he addressed Lafayette, the enthusiasm of admiration knew no bounds. The closing words of " *wel-*

come," "WELCOME," were received with a kind of rapture and the wildest excitement, that can well be imagined. Never before, and I believe, never since, was such a scene witnessed at Cambridge. And I much incline to the opinion, that for all in all, considering the occasion and the circumstances, not one of all Mr. Everett's greatest efforts, throughout his whole subsequent career, has surpassed that memorable Phi Beta oration of August 27, 1824.

In the autumn of this year, 1824, the young men of Middlesex nominated Mr. Everett for the House of Representatives in Congress. The course which he pursued in his ten years as Representative in Washington, — his services in Europe, — his administration as Governor of our State, — his presidency at Cambridge, — and even the wonderful efforts of the last glorious period of his life, — it is not now the time, nor is this the place, to review and describe. But whatever may have been thought of him, at certain times, in respect to his political action, — I believe that no man could ever say with greater sincerity and propriety, that "through good report and through evil report, he had truly loved his whole Country."

The bereavement which we mourn, is a bereavement of all the loyal people in our land. We are all mourners to-day, as if the affliction were in our own family circle. Although the beloved man had lived so long, and had accomplished so much by his integrity and learning, his patriotism and philanthropy, — and although

" gathered to his fathers," " as a shock of corn cometh in his season," his death appears to us untimely. Our duty is to bow with entire submission to God's Sovereign will. "Even so, Father, for so it seemeth good in thy sight."

Little did we think, when we so lately saw him, that he was so soon to fall asleep. But if it had been known, that his days were so near the end, and there had been the opportunity, — I think that I should have ventured to congratulate him, that God had spared him so long; and that for himself, for our land, and for the world, he was not taken from us four years since.

Grateful should we be that he so early gave himself to the pure, the beautiful, and the just. As we gather him to his burial, let us all be admonished of our personal duty to our Country and to God. I would that I could speak to all the young men of the land. I would exhort them to study those volumes which are the memorial of his erudition, his eloquence, and his beneficence.

We cannot doubt what *he* would say to them, and to all of us. And here comes to my mind, at this moment, the words which he uttered when approaching the end of that oration on the 27th of August, 1824. — " If I err in this happy vision of my Country's fortunes, I thank God for an error so animating. If this be false, may I never know the truth. Never may you, my friends, be under any other feeling than that a great and growing, an immeasurably expanding country is calling upon you for your best services.

Mr. President, there is a spot in front of this edifice, —

on the other side of that which is occupied by the statue of the great defender of the Constitution. Whose statue shall have that vacant place? Whose can occupy it so worthily as that of him whose sudden departure we all so deeply deplore?. But however it may be, it is our "joy of grief," that his monument is everywhere in the land; his renown is in all lands; and for ages to come, his Country "redeemed, regenerated, disenthralled," shall cherish among her choicest treasures, the transcendent name of EDWARD EVERETT.

Mr. Chadbourne of Berkshire said : —

MR. PRESIDENT: It is eminently proper that we should turn aside from the ordinary duties of this chamber to pay our brief tribute of respect to the memory of a great man. Edward Everett was a great man among great men. It was his lot, sir, to live and walk with a race of intellectual giants. And if we consider the rare combination of native power with vast acquirements, he was hardly surpassed by any man of his time. He was a scholar, an orator, a statesman, and a patriot. How perfect and beautiful was his life, how transcendently beautiful its close! No broken shaft can be its symbol. It was like the lofty marble column, without spot or blemish, its flutings perfect, its capital entire.

I shall ever consider it among the fortunate events in my life, sir, that I heard his last words in Faneuil Hall. There his great heart gushed forth, breaking down the forms of elaborate and studied oratory so commonly at-tributed to him. With what loving enthusiasm was he greeted by the hundreds who had so often hung upon his lips. And how did his words give us courage for the conflict and charity towards the returning prodigals. He did not live to see the Union restored, but, as has been well said, he saw it by the eye of faith. Those who heard his last speech will never forget his eloquent words respecting the people of Savannah. "They do not know as we do," said he, "that the Savannah River shall sooner reverse its course and roll its flood of waters back to the mountains than the stars and stripes be again replaced by the flag of the Rebellion." His eloquent words remain, but his eloquent lips are closed forever in death. He has completed his warfare. We may place his statue in the vacant place in front of the capitol, but his spear leans against the wall, and who is there left, mighty enough to wield it?

But how little, sir, of such a man can die! His death seems to me like one of those splendid summer nights in the far north, where the sun indeed sinks beneath the horizon, but where his midnight light curtains the heavens with purple and gold, more gorgeous and beautiful than his noonday glory.

His name will live forever. Henceforth, they who make pilgrimages to Mount Vernon will couple the name of Everett with the name of Washington. He will be remembered as the proud product of republican institutions, as the orator who launched his thunders against the Catilines of our day, and as the patriot who ever preferred his country to party, and never despaired of the republic.

The resolutions were adopted.

Senators Wentworth of Middlesex, Loud of Plymouth, Codman of Suffolk, Parker of Suffolk, Stoddard of Worcester, Frost of Norfolk, Foster of Essex, Kneil of Hampden, Ide of Bristol, and Parsons of Franklin were appointed a Committee on the part of the Senate to attend the funeral.

Adjourned.

IN THE HOUSE.

A communication was received from His Excellency, the Governor, stating that the Executive Department would unite with the General Court in any demonstration of respect to the memory of Mr. Everett, which they might adopt.

The resolutions of the joint special Committee, in relation to Mr. Everett, were received from the Senate, and read by the clerk.

Mr. Wells of Chicopee said : —

MR. SPEAKER: The brief time that remains before we are to proceed to join in the funeral ceremonies, as well as the fact that our action contemplates a formal eulogy at some future day, forbids that I should enter upon any extended discussion of the life or character of Mr. Everett. Were it otherwise, I should not venture, with my limited powers, and limited knowledge of the subject, to undertake its delineation. But I am sure it would not comport with the feelings of this house, —

it would not comport with the propriety of the occasion, that the Resolves should pass to their adoption by a mere formal vote. There is one consideration in the life of Mr. Everett, which seems especially to force itself upon our attention. Although for so many years in public life; — elected to Congress forty years ago; — having filled the office of Governor of this Commonwealth more than a quarter of a century since; — appointed in 1841 as our Minister to the Court of St. James; — in 1852 succeeding Mr. Webster as Secretary of State of the United States; — and having filled all these and other prominent positions of public trust with distinguished ability, and honor to himself as well as to the country; — he has nevertheless rounded out his life, and placed upon its record an enduring crown of surpassing excellence, by the display of that patriotism, and the performance of those duties to the country, which come within the province of the private citizen. Great and honored as he was among men when exercising the influence which attends the possession of high official position, he was greater, more honored, more powerful in the influence he was able to exert for the good of his country, in his last capacity as a private citizen.

He thus nobly illustrated the true spirit of the institutions of our country; — where the private citizen is the real potentate, — above all office, and not dependent upon it for the possession of his true dignity and influence. In the death of Mr. Everett the country has indeed suffered a great loss. And yet his life is not lost to the nation. It is fortunate for us, — fortunate in view of that immortality which is said to be possible to a nation, that its great men do not die. It is not in the power of death to tear away the life of such men from the life of the Nation. Their acts, their example, their written and spoken words, their influence upon the passing events of their time, — all that which is the expression of their lives is wrought into the public life, — woven as it were into the web of the history of the country. And although they may be withdrawn from our mortal vision, all that which was great in them, all which connects itself with the public life, remains forever. Passing time will remove whatever of cloud may be thrown upon the character by the prejudice or passion of to-day, and as we look back from some future period, we shall recognize, more fully, all that is great and good in such a life, and cherish it as a part of the national life and history.

Mr. Scudder of Dorchester said that this was not the time for an extended eulogy; the subject did not demand, nor the occasion require it. The very air was full of the praises of the illustrious dead, mingled with sighs and lamentation at his loss. He felt justified in saying, that within the last half century no man had walked among us who had so completely the characteristics of a truly great man, or whose life and character would so adorn the pages of our history. More than sixty years of the threescore and ten of his life are a history familiar to us all. The fame of his extraordinary promise as a boy still lingered in his native town of Dorchester, — a promise so wonderfully fulfilled in his after career as preacher, professor, senator, diplomate, governor, college president, and cabinet minister. Certainly Edward Everett embodied in himself all the virtues and excellences which are the components of greatness.

The resolutions were unanimously adopted, the members of the House rising in their places.

The following gentlemen were appointed by the Speaker on the Committee of the House to attend Mr. Everett's funeral : —

Messrs. Kimball of Boston, Scudder of Dorchester, Stone of Charlestown, Hills of Boston, Stone of Waltham, Gallup of Brookfield, Dwelley of Hanover, Warren of Windsor, Hall of Dennis, Holden of Salem, Bartlett of Greenfield, Lovering of Taunton, Shortle of Provincetown, Osborne of Edgartown, Mitchell of Nantucket, Stone of Lowell, Winchester of Springfield, Mudge of Petersham, Stevens of Newburyport, and Dudley of Northampton.

Adjourned.

PROCEEDINGS OF THE BOARD OF TRADE.

PROCEEDINGS OF THE BOARD OF TRADE.

A SPECIAL meeting of the Government of the Board of Trade was held on Tuesday, January 17, at noon, to consider what measures should be adopted in relation to the death of Mr. Everett. The meeting was called to order by the President, Hon. George C. Richardson, who briefly stated its objects. Edward S. Tobey, Esq. then addressed the meeting as follows : —

MR. PRESIDENT AND GENTLEMEN OF THE BOARD OF TRADE: It is but recently that this Board has had occasion to perform the solemn office of a public expression of its sense of the personal worth and eminent character of a distinguished American merchant, whose death deprived the commercial world of one of its most prominent and honored representatives. We are now summoned to this place, to bear our highest tribute of respect for the character and worth of our preëminent and revered fellow-countryman, Edward Everett, whose sudden departure has thrown the pall of sadness over our land.

Although not directly connected with the commercial history of this community, Mr. Everett has, in former years, as the able minister of the United States in Great Britain, rendered signal service to the commerce of this country, especially in giving his valuable influence in the adjustment of questions in controversy as to the rights of American Fishermen.

At an earlier date, his series of letters on the subject of our Colonial trade, doubtless had no inconsiderable influence in forming an intelligent public opinion on the commercial questions involved. Notwithstanding the grave and protracted controversy in reference to the Northeastern boundary, the Oregon question, and other kindred topics, which at one time threatened the peace of this country and of England was ultimately transferred to Washington, through the arrangement of a special ambassador from England, it is not doubted that Mr. Everett's previous discussions of those questions with the British Government largely contributed to prepare the way for the amicable settlement, which was finally attained by the commissioners of both governments.

His appointment by the government in 1843, on a mission to China, with a view to establish improved commercial relations with that country (an appointment which he felt constrained to decline), shows the estimation in which his ability on commercial questions was held.

But, Mr. President, it is not by reason of any relations to the commerce of the country which Mr. Everett sustained, that we are now convened to do appropriate honor to his memory. Our country mourns the loss of one of her ablest and most devoted statesmen; and one of Massachusetts' gifted sons, one of the great constellation of brilliant statesmen, whose lives during the last half century have adorned and illuminated the pages of our country's history, has been withdrawn from these earthly scenes.

This is, therefore, no ordinary occasion. Generally we may well be guarded against the use of words of fulsome eulogy, which too indiscriminately uttered, may alike do injury to the living and injustice to the dead.

But when one of such rare combination of virtues and excellences of character as was possessed by Mr. Everett passes from earth, we may safely commend his exemplary public and private life to the emulation of his fellow-citizens in no measured terms.

I, therefore, Mr. President, regard it both an honor and a privilege, cordially to unite with this Board in the present appropriate demonstrations of respect for the character of our deceased fellow-citizen.

Long will the tones of his matchless eloquence be treasured in memory, as with all the fervor of a pure, devoted patriotism he sought to rally the people to the standard of his country, and in support of its lawfully constituted government in its struggle with treason; or in his last pathetic appeal to the sympathies of our citizens in behalf of the suffering poor in Savannah.

But, Mr. President, I do not feel at liberty to indulge the promptings of my own heart in more extended remarks, aware, as I am, that there are others present who, I am sure, desire to give expression to their hearty approval of these proceedings. I have the honor to submit the following resolutions for your consideration : —

Resolved. That this Board would reverently acknowledge the hand of Divine Providence in the sudden departure from this life of our deeply lamented fellow-citizen, Edward Everett, whose varied public services and high attainments have been so preëminent as to make his character the common property of the American people.

Resolved. That in common with our fellow-countrymen, we share in the general sorrow which now oppresses the heart of this nation, for the irreparable loss of one whose life has adorned the brightest page of its history, and whose death has deprived the country of the wise counsel and influence of one of her noblest sons.

Resolved. That, while this Board cannot be unmindful of the eminent services rendered by Mr. Everett as the representative of his country at the Court of St. James, in his participation in the adjustment of international questions of great importance to the commercial interests of the United States, we regard it as a special privilege, not less than a solemn and sacred duty, on this sad occasion, to express our appreciation of his patriotism, his exalted and comprehensive statesmanship, and his moral worth, which, with his unsurpassed eloquence, have added lustre to the American name and character throughout the world, and will enshrine his memory in the hearts of a grateful nation.

Resolved. That we offer to his afflicted relatives and friends our sympathy in their bereavement, which has suddenly deprived them of the society of one whose affectionate intercourse and genial friendship they have been permitted so long to enjoy.

The resolutions were seconded by James M. Beebe, Esq., in the following remarks : —

MR. PRESIDENT: In rising to second the resolutions submitted, I shall but give utterance to feelings which fill the hearts of all present.

It has not been customary for this Association, a body so largely composed of merchants and business men, to publicly recognize the departure of those, however eminent or worthy, whose career and pursuits in life have been in a different sphere; but in the sad event which has called us together to-day, no precedent is needed for our guidance and action.

An occasion so fitting and proper for the full and earnest expression of the feelings of this Board, has perhaps never before occurred since our organization; and we but honor ourselves in paying the highest tributes to the exalted worth and pre-eminent talents of our fellow-citizen, whose sudden departure from us has caused universal sorrow.

Mr. Everett will be sadly missed in our own community, and the place vacated by his death cannot easily be filled. Always accessible, and ever ready on all proper occasions claiming his aid and co-operation, to render cheerful service in the furtherance of every good cause, the inexhaustible resources of his well-stored mind, and his unsurpassed eloquence were constantly sought.

His enlightened and comprehensive patriotism, his
16

noble and untiring efforts in behalf of his country and her imperilled institutions, so dear to him, have enshrined his memory in the heart of the nation, which will never forget the debt of gratitude it owes.

Little more can be expected, in our meeting to-day, than a brief recurrence to the excellence of character and efficient services of the departed. A bright example is afforded by his life, to stimulate and encourage zeal and fidelity in every good work.

Robert B. Forbes, Esq., then spoke as follows : —

MR. PRESIDENT AND GENTLEMEN: In offering my cordial support to the resolutions, my first sensation is one of regret that I cannot be endowed with a portion of the eloquence due to the occasion. If the feelings of my heart could be uttered by my lips, I might do justice to the subject.

My relations with Mr. Everett, though never very intimate, have been of the most friendly character and long standing. To no individual in this community have I been accustomed to look up with more reverence, both on account of his public works and his private character. While we sincerely mourn his departure, we cannot but rejoice that he was spared so long, and that he has gone to meet his reward, unimpaired by lingering illness, and in the fulness of his glorious career.

Who is there in this community or in the whole country, who has not been inspired to deeds of patriotism or charity by his brilliant example and unsurpassed eloquence, — who that could withstand his convincing arguments, or fail to applaud the grace of his unequalled style? None, sir, but those who have no minds to understand or no hearts to feel his power.

There are but two things to regret in Mr. Everett's death: first, that we have no one to fill his place, and next, that he could not have been spared long enough to see — what he has done so much to bring about — the restoration of our glorious Union. No man living has done more towards this end than Edward Everett; and few men, since the immortal Washington, whose lives and writings will do more, in the future, to preserve its integrity when that happy day shall come.

Mr. President, I heartily concur in the language and in the spirit of the resolutions, and in all that has been said by the gentleman who has seconded them.

Hon. Joseph M. Wightman also addressed the Board upon the adoption of the resolutions, as follows : —

MR. PRESIDENT: I desire to mingle my feelings of deep sympathy with the Board on this occasion, and to express my hearty concurrence in the resolutions, and the appropriate remarks which have been made in reference to the death of Mr. Everett.

In the various public positions with which I have been honored by my fellow-citizens, I have been brought into frequent intimate relations with Mr. Everett, and my connection, both private and official, with him, has always been characterized by a gentle courtesy, a kindly interest, and a cordial co-operation, that has entitled him to my warmest feelings of gratitude while living, and to my heartfelt sorrow and regret at his loss. But although the eloquent voice is hushed forever, and the trusty counsellor and friend has departed, we feel assured that he has only left us to repose in peace and happiness in the bosom of his God.

The resolutions were unanimously adopted.

On motion of Mr. Wightman, it was voted that the resolutions and the action of the Board in relation thereto be communicated to the family of the deceased.

Lorenzo Sabine, Secretary of the Board, offered a resolution that the rooms of the Board be draped in mourning for thirty days.

In moving its adoption, Mr. Sabine said that he, probably, was the only person now living who could do Mr. Everett full justice in a single particular, namely, while the departed statesman was negotiating the Reciprocity Treaty, as Secretary of State; and that, refraining on the present occasion, he should state the facts within his personal knowledge, at another time and in another way.

The resolution was adopted with an amendment recommending a similar demonstration in the public room of the Merchants' Exchange.

The meeting then adjourned.

PROCEEDINGS

OF THE

MASSACHUSETTS HISTORICAL SOCIETY.

PROCEEDINGS OF THE MASSACHUSETTS HISTORICAL SOCIETY.

A Special Meeting of the Massachusetts Historical Society was held in the Dowse Library on Monday evening, Jan. 30, to commemorate their late illustrious associate, Edward Everett. The attendance was very large.

The meeting was called to order at 7½ o'clock by the President, the Hon. Robert C. Winthrop, who spoke as follows : —

Gentlemen of the Massachusetts Historical Society:

The occasion of this meeting is but too well known to you all. None of us were strangers to the grief which pervaded this community on the recent announcement of the death of Edward Everett. Not a few of us have had the privilege of uniting with the public authorities, who hastened to assume the whole charge of his funeral, in paying the last tribute to his honored remains. And more than one of us have already had an opportunity of giving some feeble expression to our sense of the loss which has been sustained by our city, our Commonwealth, and our whole country.

But we are here this evening to take up the theme again somewhat more deliberately, as a Society of which he was so long one of the most valuable, as well as one of the most distinguished members. We are here not merely to unite in lamenting the close of a career which has been crowded with so many good words and good works for the community and the country at large, but to give utterance to our own particular sorrow for the breach which has been made in our own cherished circle.

Mr. Everett was elected a member of this Society on the 27th of April, 1820, when he was but twenty-six years of age; and, at the time of his death, his name stood second in order of seniority on the roll of our resident members. I need not attempt to say to you how much we have prized his companionship, how often we have profited of his counsels, or how deeply we have been indebted to him for substantial services which no one else could have rendered so well.

His earliest considerable effort in our behalf was a lecture delivered before us on the 31st of October, 1833. It was entitled " Anecdotes of Early Local History," and will be found in the second volume of his collected works, — now lying upon our table, — with an extended note or appendix containing many interesting details concerning the Society, its objects and its members. But it is only within the last nine or ten years, and since his public life — so far as office is necessary to constitute public life — was brought to a close, that he has been in the way of taking an active part in our proceedings. No one can enter the room in which we are gathered without remembering how frequently, during that period, his voice has been heard among us in rendering such honors to others, as now,

alas, we are so unexpectedly called to pay to himself.   No
one can forget his admirable tributes to the beloved Prescott, to the excellent Nathan Hale, to the venerated
Quincy, among our immediate associates ; — to Daniel D.
Barnard of Albany and Henry D. Gilpin of Philadelphia,
to Washington Irving, to Hallam, to Humboldt, to Macaulay, among our domestic and foreign honorary members.

Still less will any one be likely to forget the noble
eulogy which he pronounced, at our request, on the 9th
of December, 1858, upon that remarkable self-made man
whom we have ever delighted to honor as our largest
benefactor, and in whose pictured presence we are at this
moment assembled.   Often as I have listened to our lamented friend, since the year 1824, — when I followed
him with at least one other whom I see before me to
Plymouth Rock, and heard his splendid discourse on the
Pilgrim Fathers, — I can hardly recall anything of his,
more striking of its kind, or more characteristic of its
author, than that elaborate delineation of the life of
Thomas Dowse.   No one, certainly, who was present on
the occasion, can fail to recall the exhibition which he
gave us, in its delivery, of the grasp and precision of his
wonderful memory, — when in describing the collection
of water colors, now in the Athenæum gallery, which was
the earliest of Mr. Dowse's possessions, he repeated,
without faltering, the unfamiliar names of more than
thirty of the old masters from whose works they were
copied, and then turning at once to the description of
the library itself, as we see it now around us, proceeded
to recite the names of fifty-three of the ancient authors

17

of Greek and Roman literature, of nineteen of the modern German, of fourteen of the Italian, of forty-seven of the French, of sixteen or seventeen of the Portuguese and Spanish, making up in all an aggregate of more than one hundred and eighty names of artists and authors, many of them as hard to pronounce as they were difficult to be remembered, but which he rehearsed, without the aid of a note and without the hesitation of an instant, with as much ease and fluency as he doubtless had rolled off the famous catalogue of the ships, in the second book of Homer's Iliad, with the text-book in his hand, as a college student or as Greek professor, half a century before!

I need hardly add that with this library, now our most valued treasure, the name of Mr. Everett will henceforth be hardly less identified than that of Mr. Dowse himself. Indeed, he had been associated with it long before it was so munificently transferred to us. By placing yonder portrait of him, taken in his earliest manhood, upon the walls of the humble apartment in which the books were originally collected, — the only portrait ever admitted to their companionship, — our worthy benefactor seems himself to have designated Edward Everett as the presiding genius or patron saint of this library; and as such he will be enshrined by us, and by all who shall succeed us, as long as the precious books and the not less precious canvas shall escape the ravages of time.

I may not omit to remind you that our lamented friend — who was rarely without some labor of love for others in prospect — had at least two matters in hand for us at the time of his death, which he was hoping, and which we all were hoping, that he would soon be able to complete. One of them was a memoir of that noble patriot of South Carolina, James Louis Petigru, whose lifelong devotion to the cause of the American Union, alike in the days of nullification and of secession, will secure him the grateful remembrance of all to whom that Union is dear. The other was a volume of Washington's private letters, which he was preparing to publish in our current series of historical collections. It is hardly a month since he told me that the letters were all copied, and that he was sorry to be obliged to postpone the printing of them a little longer, in order to find time for the annotations with which he desired to accompany them.

But you do not require to be told, gentlemen, that what Mr. Everett has done, or has proposed to do, specifically for our own Society, would constitute a very small part of all that he has accomplished in that cause of American history in which we are associated. It is true that he has composed no independent historical work, nor ever published any volume of biography more considerable than the excellent memoir of Washington, which he prepared, at the suggestion of his friend Lord Macaulay, for the new edition of the Encyclopædia Britannica. But there is no great epoch, — there is hardly a single great event, — of our national or of our colonial history, which he has not carefully depicted and brilliantly illustrated in his occasional discourses. I have sometimes thought that no more attractive or more instructive history of our country could be presented to the youth of our land, than is found in the series of anniversary orations which he has delivered during the last forty years. Collect those orations into a volume by themselves; arrange them in their historical order: " The First Settlement of New England," " The Settlement of Massachusetts," " The Battle of Bloody Brook in King Philip's War," " The Seven Years' War, the School of the Revolution," " The First Battles of the Revolutionary War," " The Battle of Lexington," " The Battle of Bunker Hill," " Dorchester in 1630, 1776, and 1855;" combine with them those " Anecdotes of Early Local History," which he prepared for our own Society, and add to them his charming discourses on " The Youth of Washington," and " The Character of Washington," on " The Boyhood and the Early Days of Franklin," and his memorable eulogies on Adams and Jefferson, on Lafayette, on John Quincy Adams and on Daniel Webster, and I know not in what other volume the young men, or even the old men, of our land could find the history of the glorious past more accurately or more admirably portrayed. I know not where they could find the toils and trials and struggles of our colonial or revolutionary fathers set forth with greater fulness of detail or greater felicity of illustration. As one reads those orations and discourses at this moment, they might almost be regarded as successive chapters of a continuous and comprehensive work which had been composed and recited on our great national anniversaries, just as the chapters of Herodotus are said to have been recited at the Olympic festivals of ancient Greece.

Undoubtedly, however, it is rather as an actor and an

orator in some of the later scenes of our country's history, than as an author, that Mr. Everett will be longest remembered. Indeed, since he first entered on the stage of mature life, there has hardly been a scene of any sort in that great historic drama, which of late, alas, has assumed the most terrible form of tragedy, in which he has not been called to play a more or less conspicuous part; and we all know how perfectly every part which has been assigned him has been performed. If we follow him from the hour when he left the University of Cambridge, with the highest academic honors, at an age when so many others are hardly prepared to enter there, down to the fatal day when he uttered those last impressive words at Faneuil Hall, we shall find him everywhere occupied with the highest duties, and everywhere discharging those duties with consummate ability and unwearied devotion. Varied and brilliant accomplishments, laborious research, copious diction, marvellous memory, magnificent rhetoric, a gracious presence, a glorious voice, an ardent patriotism controlling his public career, an unsullied purity crowning his private life, — what element was there wanting in him for the complete embodiment of the classic orator, as Cato and Quinctilian so tersely and yet so comprehensively defined him eighteen hundred years ago — " *Vir bonus, dicendi peritus !* "

But I may not occupy more of your time in these introductory remarks, intended only to exhibit our departed friend in his relations to our own Society, and to open the way for those who are prepared to do better justice to his general career and character. Let me only add that our standing committee have requested our associates, Mr. Hillard and Dr. Lothrop, to prepare some appropriate resolutions for the occasion, and that the Society is now ready to receive them.

Mr. Hillard then proceeded as follows : —

The Psalmist says, " The days of our years are three-score years and ten, and if by reason of strength they be fourscore years, yet is their strength, labor and sorrow." The latter part of this sentence is not altogether true ; at least, it is not without exceptions as numerous as the rule. To say nothing of the living, we who have witnessed the serene and beautiful old age of Quincy, protracted more than twenty years after threescore years and ten, will not admit that all of life beyond that limit is of necessity " labor and sorrow." But in these words there is much of truth as this, that he who has lived to be threescore and ten years old should feel that he has had his fair share of life, and if any more years are dropped into his lap he must receive them as a gift not promised at his birth. And thus no man who dies after the age of seventy can be said to have died unseasonably or prematurely. But the shock with which the news of Mr. Everett's death fell upon the community was due to its unexpectedness as well as its suddenness. We knew that he was an old man, but we did not feel that he was such. There was nothing either in his aspect or his life that warned us of departure or reminded us of decay. His powers were so vigorous, his industry was so great, his sympathies were so active, his eloquence was so rich and glowing, his elocution still so admirable, that he appeared before us as a man in the very prime of life, and when he died it was as if the sun had gone down at noon. The impression made by his death was the highest tribute that could be paid to the worth of his life.

In 1819, after an absence of nearly five years, Mr. Everett returned from Europe at the age of twenty-five, the most finished and accomplished man that had been seen in New England, and it will be generally admitted that he maintained this superiority to the last. From that year down to the hour of his death he was constantly before the public eye, and never without a marked and peculiar influence upon the community, especially upon students and scholars. You and I, Mr. President, are old enough to have come under the spell of the magician at that early period of his life, when he presented the most attractive combination of graceful and blooming youth with mature intellectual power. The young man of to-day, familiar with that expression of gravity, almost of sadness, which his countenance has habitually worn of late, can hardly imagine what he then was, when his " bosom's lord sat light upon his throne," when the winds of hope filled his sails, and his looks and movements were informed with a spirit of morning freshness and vernal promise.

In the forty-five years which passed between his return home and his death, Mr. Everett's industry was untiring, and the amount of work he accomplished was immense. What he published would alone entitle him to the praise of a very industrious man, but this forms but a part of his labors. Of what has been called the master-vice of sloth he knew nothing. He was independent of the amusements and relaxations which most hard-working men interpose between their hours of toil. He was always in harness.

Some persons have regretted that he gave so much time to merely occasional productions, instead of devoting himself to some one great work; but without speculating upon the comparative value of what we have and what we might have had, it is enough to say that with his genius and temperament on the one hand, and our institutions and form of society on the other, it was a sort of necessity that his mind should have taken the direction that it did. For he was the child of his time, and was always in harmony with the spirit of the age and country in which his lot was cast. He was pre-eminently rich in the fruits of European culture; Greece, Rome, England, France, Italy, and Germany, all helped by liberal contributions to swell his stores of intellectual wealth, but yet no man was ever more national in feeling, more patriotic in motive and impulse, more thoroughly American in grain and fibre. Loving books as he did, he would yet have pined and languished if he had been doomed to live in the unsympathetic air of a great library. The presence, the comprehension, the sympathy of his kind were as necessary to him as his daily bread.

"Two words," says Macaulay, "form the key of the Baconian doctrine, Utility and Progress." I think these two words also go far to reveal and interpret Mr.

Everett's motives and character. Not that he did not seek honorable distinction, not that he did not take pleasure in the applause which he had fairly earned; but stronger even than these propelling impulses was his desire to be of service to his fellowmen, to do good in his day and generation. He loved his country with a fervid love, and he loved his race with a generous and comprehensive philanthropy. He was always ready to work cheerfully in any direction when he thought he could do any good, though the labor might not be particularly congenial to his tastes, and would not add anything to his literary reputation. The themes which he handled, during his long life of intellectual action, were very various, they were treated with great affluence of learning, singular beauty of illustration, and elaborate and exquisite harmony of style, but always in such a way as to bear practical fruit, and contribute to the advancement of society and the elevation of humanity.

So, too, Mr. Everett was a sincere and consistent friend of progress. He was, it is true, conservative in his instincts and convictions; I mean in a large and liberal, and not in a narrow and technical sense. But that he was an extreme conservative, or that he valued an institution simply because it was old, is not only not true, but, I think, the reverse of truth. He had a distaste to extreme views of any kind, and, by the constitution of his mind, was disposed to take that middle ground which partisan zeal is prone to identify with timidity or indifference. But he was a man of

18

generous impulses and large sympathies. No one was more quick to recognize true progress, and greet it with a more hospitable welcome. No man of his age would have more readily and heartily acknowledged the many points in which the world has advanced since he was young.

It would not be seasonable here to dwell upon Mr. Everett's public or political career, but I may be permitted to add that I think he had genuine faith in the institutions of his country, which did not grow fainter as he grew older. He believed in man's capacity for self-government, and had confidence in popular instincts. He was fastidious in his social tastes, but not aristocratic; that is, if he preferred one man to another it was for essential and not adventitious qualities, for what they were, and not for what they had. He was uniformly kind to the young, and always prompt to recognize and encourage merit in a young person.

Mr. Everett, if not the founder of the school of American deliberative eloquence, was its most brilliant representative. In his orations and occasional discourses will be found his best title to remembrance, and by them his name will surely be transmitted to future generations. In judging of them, we must bear in mind that the aim of the deliberative orator is to treat a subject in such a way as to secure and fix the attention of a popular audience, and this aim Mr. Everett never lost sight of. If it be said that his discourses are not marked by originality of construction, or philosophical depth of thought, it may be replied that had they been so, they would have been less attractive to his hearers. They are remarkable for a combination of qualities rarely, if ever before, so happily blended, and especially for the grace, skill, and tact with which the resources of the widest cultivation are so used as to instruct the common mind and touch the common heart. For, whatever were the subject, Mr. Everett always took his audience along with him, from first to last. He never soared or wandered out of their sight.

I need not dwell upon the singular beauty and finish of his elocution. Those who have heard him speak will need no description of the peculiar charm and grace of his manner, and no description will give any adequate impression of it to those who never heard him. It was a manner easily caricatured but not easily imitated. His power over an audience remained unimpaired to the last. At the age of seventy he spoke with all the animation of youth, and easily filled the largest hall with that rich and flexible voice, the tones of which time had hardly touched.

His organization was delicate and refined, his temperament was sensitive and sympathetic. The opinion of those whom he loved and esteemed was weighty with him. Praise was ever cordial to him, and more necessary than to most men who had achieved such high and assured distinction. Doubtful as the statement may seem to those who knew him but slightly, or only saw him on the platform with his " robes and singing garlands " about him, he was to the last a modest and self-distrustful man. He never appeared in public without a slight flutter of apprehension lest he should fall short of that standard which he had created for himself. His want of self-confidence, and, in later years, his want of animal spirits, sometimes produced a coldness of manner, which, by superficial observers, was set down to coldness of heart, but most unjustly.

His nature was courteous, gentle, and sweet. Few men were ever more worthy than he to wear "the grand old name of gentleman." His manners were graceful, more scholarly than is usual with men who had been so much in public life as he, and sometimes covered with a delicate veil of reserve. Conflict and contest were distasteful to him, and it was his disposition to follow the things that make for peace. He had a true respect for the intellectual rights of others, and it was no fault of his if he ever lost a friend through difference of opinion.

Permit me to turn for a moment to Mr. Everett's public life for an illustration of his character. In forensic contests, sarcasm and invective are formidable and frequent weapons. The House of Commons quailed before the younger Pitt's terrible powers of sarcasm. An eminent living statesman and orator of Great Britain is remarkable for both these qualities. But neither invective nor sarcasm is to be found in Mr. Everett's speeches. I think this absence is to be ascribed not to an intellectual want but to a moral grace.

Great men, public men, have also their inner and private life, and sometimes this must be thrown by the honest painter into shadow. But in Mr. Everett's case there was no need of this, for his private life was spotless. In conduct and conversation he always conformed to the highest standard which public opinion exacts of the members of that profession to which he originally belonged. As a brother, husband, father, and friend, there was no duty that he did not discharge, no call that he did not obey. He was generous in giving, and equally generous in sacrificing. Where he was most known he was best loved. He was wholly free from that exacting temper in small things which men, eminent and otherwise estimable, sometimes fall into. His daily life was made beautiful by a pervading spirit of thoughtful consideration for those who stood nearest to him. His household manners were delightful, and his household discourse was brightened by a lambent play of wit and humor; qualities which he possessed in no common measure, though they were rarely displayed before the public. Could the innermost circle of Mr. Everett's life be revealed to the general eye, it could not fail to deepen the sense of bereavement which his death has awakened, and to increase the reverence with which his memory is and will be cherished.

No man ever bore his faculties and his eminence more meekly than he. He never declined the lowly and commonplace duties of life. He was always approachable and accessible. The constant and various interruptions to which he was exposed by the innumerable calls made upon his time and thoughts were borne by him with singular patience and sweetness.

His industry was as methodical as it was uniform. However busy he might be, he could always find time for any service which a friend required at his hands. He was scrupulously faithful and exact in small things. He never broke an appointment or a promise. His splendid powers worked with all the regularity and precision of the most nicely adjusted machinery. If he had undertaken to have a discourse, a report, an article, ready at a certain time, it might be depended upon as surely as the rising of the sun.

I feel that I have hardly touched upon the remarkable qualities of Mr. Everett's mind and character, and yet I have occupied as much of your time as is becoming. I have only to offer a few resolutions, in which I have endeavored briefly and simply to give expression to what we all feel.

Mr. Hillard then presented the following resolutions : —

Resolved, That as members of the Massachusetts Historical Society, we record, with mingled pride and sorrow, our sense of what we have lost in the death of our late illustrious associate, Edward Everett, the wise statesman, the eloquent orator, the devoted patriot, the finished scholar, whose long life of singular and unbroken intellectual activity has shed new lustre upon the name of our country in every part of the civilized world, and whose noble powers and unrivalled accomplishments were always inspired by an enlarged and enlightened philanthropy, and dedicated to the best interests of knowlege, virtue, and truth.

Resolved, That we recall with peculiar sensibility the personal qualities and private virtues of our departed friend, the purity and beauty of his daily life, his strict allegiance to duty, the strength and tenderness of his domestic affections, the uniform conscientiousness which regulated his conduct, his spirit of self-sacrifice, his thoughtful consideration for the rights and happiness of others, and the gentleness with which his great faculties and high honors were borne.

Resolved, That the President of the Society be requested to transmit these resolutions to the family of our lamented associate, with an expression of our deep sympathy with them in their loss, and of our trust that they may find consolation not merely in the remembrance of his long, useful, and illustrious career, but in the hopes and promises of that religion of which he was a firm believer, and which was ever to him a staff of support through life.

The resolutions were seconded by Rev. Dr. Lothrop, who then addressed the meeting, as follows : —

Mr. President : I rise, at your request and at that of the standing committee, to second the resolutions which have just been offered, and to pay my portion of the tribute of profound, grateful, and affectionate respect, which the Society would offer this evening to the memory of our eminent deceased associate. And as we gather within these walls and in this room, where we have so often welcomed his presence, I feel brought back upon me afresh that sense of loneliness and of personal bereavement, which, in common with so many, I had when I first heard that one who for more than forty years had been the object of my youthful and my mature admiration, one whose speech never disappointed me, but had often stirred my heart with pure and noble emotions, and to whom I and others had so long been accustomed to turn upon all occasions of public interest and importance, as the person who could do and say, in the best way, the best things to be done and said, was really dead, and that the utterances of his wisdom and eloquence would never more be heard by us on earth. My sorrow, however, at his departure, the sorrow of all of us, I think, must be greatly softened by the extraordinary felicity of the time and manner of his death, and by the recollection of the grand and noble career of which that death was the close.

In view of my profession and the pulpit which it has been my honor and happiness to occupy in this city, it may be permitted me, in glancing at his career, to speak with some particularity of that which was the beginning of it before the public — his brief but honorable connection with the clerical profession, and his short but brilliant pastorate at Brattle Street Church. Mr. Everett has said, I believe, that on leaving college his strongest preferences were for the law; but the influence and advice of friends, combining with the promptings of his own heart, the deep religious instincts of his nature, determined his choice of the Christian ministry. That determination must now be regarded as fortunate for him and for us. He left the pulpit, indeed, shortly after he had entered it; but no true man ever forgets that he has stood in it, and the studies, the spiritual discipline and culture of his early profession seem to me to have exerted upon Mr. Everett's mind and heart blessed and important influences, which affected his whole subsequent career, and impregnated his life and character with the simple but grand dignity of purity. Graduating in 1811, at the age of seventeen, he spent two years and a few months at Cambridge, pursuing theological studies, and discharging at the same time the onerous duties of a tutorship. On the 10th of December, 1813, a mere youth, who had not yet numbered twenty winters, he first stood in Brattle Street pulpit to preach as a candidate. Fame had preceded him, and told of his talents rich and rare, of his great learning and his great capacity to learn, — marvellous even then in the judgment of his peers and of the University, — of his extraordinary gift of golden speech, his powers of winning, persuasive oratory.

The great, though vague and undefined expectations thus awakened, were not disappointed. I have been told by many who distinctly remember the occasion, that when he rose in the pulpit that morning, a youthful modesty, almost timidity, blending with the dignity which a grave and reverent sense of the importance of his office inspired, lent a fascinating charm to his manner, and that from the moment he opened his lips, the audience were held spellbound to the end of the service. When the days of his engagement were numbered, the universal cry was, "Come unto us in the name of the Lord; break unto us the bread of life, and let all these rich gifts find their usefulness and their glory in the service of the Master here among us."

19

He heard the cry as the leadings of Providence, and came. His ordination, on the 9th of February, 1814, was an occasion of as deep interest as any event of the kind ever excited. The most eminent and excellent men of that day took part in it. It brought a perfect satisfaction to the people. It awakened the most brilliant anticipations. It was accompanied not simply with the hope, but with the conviction, that the former glory of that pulpit, which the death of Buckminster had veiled for a season, would be revived with increased and increasing splendor. That conviction was verified. As the months rolled on, Brattle Street Church, then near the residences rather than the business of the people, was crowded Sunday after Sunday with audiences of the intelligent and the cultivated, who went away charmed, instructed, religiously impressed; and the records of the communion show that it was a season of spiritual growth as well as of outward prosperity. But the year had not reached its close before painful rumors began to prevail that this was not to last, and at the end of thirteen months after his ordination, he resigned his charge, to accept the Eliot Professorship of Greek Literature in the University at Cambridge, to which he had been appointed by the corporation, with leave of study and travel for five years in Europe, in further preparation for its duties.

He left the clerical profession, and virtually the pulpit, when he thus left Brattle Street Church. On his return from Europe, indeed, and for two or three years subsequent, he preached occasionally, some ten or fifteen, perhaps twenty times in all. I may be permitted a brief allusion to some of these occasions, which I remember. First, of course, he preached in what had been his own pulpit, Brattle Street, in the summer of 1819, a few weeks after his return. I was one of the mighty company that thronged the aisles of that church on that day, and, standing on the window-seat nearest the door in the north gallery, heard him for the first time when I was just old enough to receive my first idea of eloquence, to understand and feel something of its power. A month or two later, in December of that year, I think, he preached a famous Christmas sermon at King's Chapel, and on the first Sunday in December, 1820, the Quarterly Charity Lecture, at the Old South Church, which was crowded to overflowing to hear him. Another memorable and impressive sermon of his, preached several times in different pulpits in this vicinity, and which several gentlemen present must distinctly remember, was on the text, " The time is short." He preached the sermon at the funeral of the Rev. Dr. Bently, of Salem, on the 3d of January, 1820, President Kirkland and Dr. Ware of the University officiating in the other parts of the service. This arrangement was probably made in the expectation that Dr. Bently had left his valuable library to Harvard College. But the doctorate from Cambridge was conferred too late, and it was found that the library had been bequeathed to Alleghany College; so, to the deep regret of those who heard it, Mr. Everett's sermon on this occasion was never published. On the 19th of January, 1821, he preached the sermon at the dedication of the First Congregational Church in the city of New York, of which the late Rev.

Wm. Ware subsequently became pastor. This sermon was published, and is, I believe, the only sermon he ever published. It is the only one I have ever seen. In style it is simple and grave, less rhetorical than his orations. It is liberal, but conservative, in its theology, broad and catholic in its charity, fervent in tone and spirit, evidently the product of a devout heart. This dedication at New York was the last or among the last occasions on which he preached. I feel quite confident that he did not preach after 1821, because the next year, as some who hear me will remember, in addition to the lectures connected with his professorship, and other duties at Cambridge, he was occupied with a course of lectures, whose preparation, judging from their learning and brilliancy, must have cost him no little time and study, on Art and Architecture, — more especially, if my memory serves me, on Greek and Egyptian Architecture, — which he delivered at what was then called the Pantheon Hall, on Washington Street, a little south of the Boylston Market. Lectures of this kind were then unusual in Boston, and these, having in addition to their novelty, the strong attraction of the name and fame of the lecturer, were attended by an audience as cultivated and appreciative as ever assembled for a similar purpose.

From this review it appears that his whole connection with the pulpit, including his preparatory studies and pastorate before he went to Europe, and the period during which he preached occasionally after his return, was only about five years. His exclusive connection with it as pastor was only one year and a month lacking four days, from the 9th of February, 1814, to the 5th of March 1815. In this brief period he made an impression, as a preacher, which abides distinct and clear to this hour in many hearts. He left the pulpit with the reputation of being the most eminent and eloquent man in it; and he left in and with the profession one book — his " Defence of Christianity "— which at the time it was published was justly regarded as one of the most learned and important theological works that had then been written in America, and which, considering its contents, the circumstances under which it was prepared, and the extreme youth of the author, may still be regarded as one of the most extraordinary books produced at any time in any profession. It is one of those books, of which the paradox may be uttered, that its success caused its failure. It so perfectly accomplished its work that it almost dropt out of existence. Few of the present generation ever heard of it, fewer still know anything about it. Copies of it can now be found only here and there, on the shelves of Public Libraries, or among the books of aged clergymen. It was prepared, as some gentlemen here will remember, in reply to a work by Mr. George Bethune English, who graduated at Cambridge in 1807, the year Mr. Everett entered. This gentleman, not without talents, but erratic in his career, which his death terminated in 1828, remained at Cambridge four or five years after graduating, studied theology, and I believe, preached for a brief period. Being led, apparently by the study of the deistical works of Anthony

Collins, to adopt opinions unfavorable to Christianity as
a divine revelation, he published a book entitled, "The
Grounds of Christianity examined by comparing the
New Testament with the Old." This work, plausible in
spirit, having the appearance of great candor in statement and fairness in argument, attracted attention and
was much read. It unsettled the faith of many, and,
if left unanswered, seemed destined to do this for many
more.

Mr. Everett did, what several older men, I have
heard, attempted without success; he made a triumphant
answer to Mr. English's book, in a volume of nearly
five hundred pages, which to this day must be regarded
as replete with the learning bearing upon its particular point. Cogent in argument, clear and close in its
reasoning, eloquent often in the fervor and glow of a
devout faith, keen yet kind in its wit and satire, conclusive in its exposition of the ignorance of his opponent,
his plagiarism, and his dishonesty in the use of his materials, this book so completely extinguished Mr. English
and his disciples, that it soon ceased to be read itself.
It died out, as I have said, and is now known only to
a few of the older members of the community and the
profession. It is a book of such a character, that any
man at any period of his life might be pardoned the
manifestation of some little self-complacency at finding
himself the author of it. Many have passed a long
life in the profession, and held a high and honorable
position in it, without giving any evidence of the

mastery of so much of the learning that belongs to it as is contained in this work.

His " Defence of Christianity," written partly before his ordination and published six months afterwards, in August, 1814, was Mr. Everett's legacy to the clerical profession, bequeathed to it before he was invested with a legal manhood. I am aware that their opinions on the Prophets and the Old Testament, generally, do not permit some eminent theological scholars to put a very high estimate upon Mr. Everett's " Defence of Christianity," but, for myself, without disparagement of the good he has done, and the honors he has attained in other departments, I cannot but think, that if there be any one event, work, or labor of his varied and useful life, of which he may, on a just estimate of things, be most proud, it is that in the days of his early youth, on the very threshold of his career, he prepared and published this book, which silenced the voice of infidelity and gave peace, satisfaction, and a firm faith to thousands of minds in a young and growing community.

We are not surprised that a career, which began in such industry, in the exhibition of so much learning and such fidelity in improving opportunity, should have gone on to the close increasing in honor and usefulness. I do not propose to follow this career with such minuteness all through, nor would it be proper in me to do so here; but as I have spoken of the clergyman, I may be permitted to say something of the Professor at Cambridge, as I am the only member of the Society present, who, as a pupil in the Academic Department of the University, had the benefit of his instructions and lectures. Cambridge and the family of President Kirkland having been my home for several years before I entered college in 1821, not long after he entered upon his professorship, I knew something about the college, and had ample opportunity of knowing also the fresh impulse which he gave to the study of Greek, by the general influence of his reputation as a Greek scholar, by his occasional presence at our recitations to the tutors in Greek, by his suggestive directions or advice to such students as wished to give special attention to this department, but chiefly by his lectures on the Greek language and literature, which were delivered to the senior class, in what was then, there being three, the second or Spring Term of the college year. The class graduating in 1825, of which I was a member, was the last of the six classes who had the benefit of these lectures. From my recollection of them, from notes taken at the time, and from the printed synopsis which was furnished for our guidance, I have a strong impression of the extraordinary character of those lectures, as profound, comprehensive, discriminating, and largely exhaustive of all the learning connected with their theme. Had he published them when he resigned, he would have left in his Professor chair a legacy as remarkable, in its kind, as his legacy to the pulpit in his " Defence of Christianity," and secured to himself such a reputation as a Greek scholar, master of all the learning appertaining to the history and criticism of Greek literature, as many a man would have been willing to rest upon for the remainder of his life.

But while professor at Cambridge, Mr. Everett was interested not simply in his immediate duties, but in whatever touched the welfare and improvement of the college. In all departments his influence was felt, and in one direction he was active in a way which had some connection, I suppose, with his resignation of his professorship to enter upon political life. In 1823, some of the eminent gentlemen at Cambridge, then resident professors, took up the thought, not without some quite substantial reasons, that the " Fellows," as they are termed in the Charter, " Members of the Corporation," as we commonly designate them, should be chosen from among themselves; that the authoritative body, controlling the college, having primarily the charge of all its interests, and the conduct of all its affairs, should be composed of the working men on the spot, who best understood its condition and its wants, and were most competent to carry it on successfully, rather than of gentlemen engaged in other occupations, and living in Boston, Salem, or some more distant place. In 1824, they prepared a memorial to this effect, addressed to the Corporation, who referred them to the Board of Overseers, before which body, a hearing, asked for and granted, was subsequently held. The late Andrews Norton, Dexter Professor of Sacred Literature, and Mr. Everett, were selected to represent the memorialists at this hearing. Mr. Norton read a very able paper, marked by the concise accuracy of statement and closeness of reasoning for which he was distinguished. Mr. Everett without manuscript, with only a few brief memoranda, such as a lawyer

20

would use before a jury, addressed the Board in a speech occupying more than two hours. He was interrupted at times by gentlemen of the Board adverse to the position of the memorialists, the accuracy, a pertinence, or propriety of his statements questioned, and in one instance, if not more, the decision of the Chair, (Lieut. Gov. Morton presiding,) that he was " not in order," required him to change his line of argument and remark. Nothing, however, seemed to confuse or discompose him. The situation was novel and trying, yet he sustained himself with an admirable degree of self-possession, and conducted his cause with great ability. I have always supposed that it was the exhibition of his powers on this occasion, the coolness and tact with which he conducted himself in an argument, and sometimes almost a debate, before a body of eminent men, some of whom were opposed to his position, that first suggested his nomination to represent Middlesex in Congress, and that his splendid and eloquent oration before the Phi Beta Kappa Society, in August, 1824, only helped to confirm the purpose of his nomination, and secure his election. Thus much at least is clear, any distrust that may have been felt in any quarter as to his fitness or competency for congressional service, in view of his scholastic training and habits, found a conclusive answer in the manner in which he bore himself in this hearing before the Board of Overseers.

But whatever suggested the nomination, it was made, and he was elected in the autumn of 1824, and, delivering his lectures for the last time in the spring of 1825, he

resigned and took his seat in Congress in December of
that year. The deep regret felt and expressed by many
at that time, that so much learning, such various abilities,
persuasive eloquence, and rare combination of qualities,
were lost to the direct service of literature and religion,
must be largely diminished, if not entirely extinguished by
his eminent and brilliant success, by his wide-spread usefulness in varied departments of public and political life,
by the singular nobleness and purity of his whole career,
and by his constant fidelity and devotedness to the interests
of truth, virtue, and religion. For he seems to me to have
been thus faithful and devoted. I feel disposed to maintain that Mr. Everett was true always to the spirit of his
early vows, and though he did not continue in the administration of religion as an institution of society, he
continued to cultivate its spirit and power in his heart,
and to make it the controlling inspiration and energy of
his life. It is not necessary, nor would it be proper for
me here, to go into an analysis of his speeches, votes,
or conduct at various junctures in our public affairs during
the last forty years, but it seems to me, that whatever
difference of judgment party predilections may dispose us
to entertain about portions of his public career, a broad,
generous, just, and fair review of the whole of it, will lead
every one to concur in the position, that it was all under-
laid and impregnated from the beginning to the end with
a simple, honest, conscientious, patriotic purpose. The
very admirable and beautiful analysis of his character,
which Mr. Hillard has just read before us, seemed to me
to confirm this position, and to give the true explanation

of his course. From his entrance upon public life in 1825, to the spring of 1861, all through those more than thirty years, in which the struggle between the antagonistic elements of liberty and slavery in our government and institutions came up in various forms, he, in common with many of our greatest statesmen and large masses of our people, felt that a certain line of policy was the wisest and the best, most adapted to keep the peace, to preserve the Union from dissolution, and the Government and the country from ruin. Therefore, adhering to this policy, adopted on conviction, he was for patience, forbearance, compromise, concession, for yielding anything and everything that could, not simply in justice, but in generosity and honor, be yielded to satisfy those who were perpetually holding over us the menace of dissolution. Honestly, and in the spirit of a broad patriotism, to disarm this menace of all occasion and all justification, was the purpose of his action and policy while in public office, and of his efforts as a private citizen, and especially of that grand national pilgrimage which he made with the life and character of Washington as the theme of a magnificent discourse, which he delivered so many times to such vast assemblies in all the principal cities of the land, in the hope that under the shadow of that august name, and by the glory of a memory so sacred to all of us, he might allay sectional prejudice and the strife of parties, and bind all together in a common love and devotion to the Union. But when this hope failed, and he found that treason had developed its plans, that rebellion, unfurling its standard, had inaugurated civil war, then the policy that had hitherto guided his life was instantly abandoned. He felt that there was no longer any room for concession or compromise, and so gave himself, time, talents, wisdom, strength, all that he had, in all the ways that he could, to support the legitimate Government of the United States, in all the action and policy by which that Government sought to maintain at all hazards and at any cost the integrity of the Union and country which that Government was instituted to preserve. But in all this he was under the inspiration of a patriotism that always dwelt in his heart, though in these latter years he seems to have been raised to an energy, enthusiasm, and earnestness of effort, that indicate a deeper and stronger conviction that he was right than he exhibited or perhaps ever experienced before.

This is the true interpretation, I conceive, to be put upon Mr. Everett's political course as a public man. In our estimate of him intellectually, it will not be maintained, I presume, that Mr. Everett was one of those grand, original, creative, inventive, productive minds, that strike out new paths in science, philosophy, or the policies of States. Such minds come upon the world only in the cycle of centuries. But he had a mind of vast powers, capable of comprehending principles, gathering up details, and making use of both. He had a conscientious, unwearied industry, and consequently accumulated vast stores of knowledge in all the departments of art, science, history, and literature. He had a wonderful memory, raised to its highest power by constant culture and exercise. He had a rare combination of intellectual, moral, and physical faculties, and above all, he had the power of using all his faculties and all his acquisitions with grace, beauty, and dignity, so that he touched nothing that he did not illustrate and adorn, and came before us ever, on all occasions, with a freshness and force that charmed and instructed. As is well known to his intimate friends, he was singularly kind, tender, faithful, and true in every domestic relation of life, and to all the claims of kindred and friendship, with a warm heart under a reserved manner, and a sympathizing spirit under lips often reticent; and if, remembering this, we do justice to his private, personal character, and then look at his public career, at the wide circle of varied offices which he successively held, at the labor performed, the ability displayed in each; if we add to these his works as a scholar and a literary man, — his magnificent orations, all of them such masterpieces of eloquence, pure and elevating in their impression; broad, noble, generous in their thoughts; breathing ever the spirit of piety and patriotism, fitted to instruct our people and unfold our history, while they adorn our literature,— his numerous contributions to the periodical press, especially those to the *North American Review*, often profound discussions of grave questions in literature and philosophy; if we then crown all with the noble and patriotic labors of the last four years, we find enough surely in this survey to win for him alike our admiration and our gratitude; enough, and more than enough, to dispose us to bow before his memory in reverence, and accord to him the name and the fame of being a great man. Where shall we find one who in such varied spheres has done so much and done it so well? His was a noble life and character, and his career, followed from the beginning to the end, was marvellous in its early precocity, its growing wisdom, its ever increasing breadth, and its grand conclusion. He was a Franklin Medal scholar in the old North Grammar School at the age of ten, a Franklin Medal scholar at the Public Latin School at thirteen, chief in his class at Cambridge at seventeen, a tutor in the University at eighteen, an ordained minister of the Gospel before he was twenty, appointed to a professorship of Greek literature before he was twenty-one, elected a member of Congress at thirty; and thence, after a few years' service in the halls of national legislation, he was called to the Chief Magistracy of this State, all of whose affairs he directed with wisdom, dignity, and usefulness, — and thence to represent his country abroad in one of its most important and honorable foreign embassies, — and thence, on his return to his native land, to preside over the interests of learning at its oldest and most advanced University, — and thence to a seat in the National Cabinet for the Department of State, — and thence to a place in that august body, the Senate of the United States, — and thence, through noble and patriotic labors, to a higher and broader place than he had ever held before, in the hearts of his countrymen; and when he had attained to this grand preëminence, to be the foremost private citizen in all the land, holding no public office, but wielding a power and doing a service which mere office could never do, wearing this great distinction with unaffected modesty, walking among us with none of the infirmities but all the glory of age upon his person, and the wisdom of age in his speech, — then the beautiful and fitting end came, and without a lingering sickness, without a shadow upon his noble faculties, suddenly he died. Alone in his solitary preëminence, alone, as it were, he died; and that cold Sunday morning air, that brought a chill to our bodies, as it swept through our streets and by our doors with its sad announcement, " Edward Everett is dead!" brought a chill to our hearts which the warmth of many summers will not dispel, and left an image and a memory there that will abide with all of us, beautiful and bright, so long as we live. Mr. President, I second the resolutions.

The Hon. John C. Gray then spoke as follows : —

Mr. President: Apart from the intimation with which I have been honored through you and other respected friends, I might have been prompted by my own feelings to offer a few remarks on this most solemn and interesting occasion. One of the few remaining companions of my youth has departed. An uninterrupted friendship of nearly sixty years has been dissolved. But I am not here to speak of my own loss or my own feelings, but to contribute in doing justice to the memory of the deceased. The theme is a most copious one. It is not my purpose to analyze the character of our friend, still less to indulge in vague and extravagant eulogy. I prefer to speak briefly of those points in his character which have stamped themselves most deeply on my own memory. We were of the same class in college, and for two years of our college life occupied the same apartment. I have ever looked back on that association as one of the most valuable, as well as one of the most gratifying, of my early days. His ripeness of judgment was not less remarkable than the precocity of his genius. But there is yet higher praise.

I can say, and you perceive that I had some means of knowing, that I never knew one who preserved a more unruffled temper. Not a single instance can I recollect of irritability. Such a temper must of necessity be its own reward, and I think we may fairly ascribe to it much of his subsequent greatness. For, sir, among the many weighty truths which fell from his lips, I recollect none more striking than a remark in his lecture to the working-men, while recommending the improvement of their leisure hours. " Generally speaking," he observes, " our business allows us time enough, if our passions would but spare us." Never man more faithfully practised as he preached. In the course of his life he had his share of those chastening dispensations which come in various shapes and degrees to every one. But none of them caused the slightest remission in his unwearied industry. The great summons which awaits us all found him at his work, and so it would have done, come when it might. I shall say little more of his college life. New England education was not then what it has since become. Mr. Everett improved his literary advantages to the utmost, and bore off the first honors.

21

I pass over his short but brilliant ministry in the pulpit and his years of assiduous study in foreign countries. Shortly after his return he assumed the post of editor of our leading review. It was at a most interesting period. This country and Great Britain had closed their contests by an honorable peace, and there was on our side a general disposition to cultivate a friendly and respectful feeling towards our late adversaries. This certainly was not fully reciprocated. The leading British reviews seemed to agree in nothing so much as in speaking of our country and its institutions with hatred or contempt. Mr. Everett felt it his duty to stand forth in defence of our good name. It is not a little to his praise that while he did this most ably and earnestly, he always preserved the dignity befitting his cause and himself, and never descended to meet his antagonists with their own weapons. There is good reason to believe that his candid and manly appeals to the good sense of the people of England were not in vain, and that they contributed to create among educated Englishmen a feeling better becoming them and more just to us, a feeling which for a long time seemed prevalent, and which we had hoped would have been general and permanent. Mr. Everett's able and eloquent defences of the good name of his country naturally led to invitations to serve her in public trusts.

I will not pretend to say that such invitations were unacceptable. Suffice it to remark that, if he desired public life, he never accepted an office which was not properly offered, never purchased one by pledges in advance, direct or indirect, and never for a moment used his position for the emolument of himself or his friends. What I have more to say will be devoted to his personal character. A spotless private character has ever been considered in New England, and I trust not in New England alone, as one of the elements of true greatness, and Heaven forbid that it should ever be held in light estimation! This merit was his beyond impeachment, — not his alone, most certainly, but his eminence in other respects rendered his example in this more conspicuous, and thus more widely beneficial. Of this character I shall notice one leading feature, — I mean his wakeful and unremitted disposition to benefit others. If judged by his fruits, we must allow that Edward Everett was a most benevolent man, His exertions and resources of mind, body, or estate were most freely imparted on every reasonable call, — I should say on every reasonable opportunity. Whether the applicant was a friend or a stranger, the occasion conspicuous or unconspicuous, it was enough for him that he could serve or oblige in great or small. And now, sir, I will close by a few inquiries. No one will suspect me of disparaging any of our eminent men, departed or surviving, when I ask —

Has any one among us ever been more distinguished by a noble use of noble endowment? Has there been any one less obnoxious to the charge of talents wasted and time misspent, any one who could say with more truth in words he once felt compelled to utter, that he knew not how the bread of idleness tasted? Has any one done more, by his wise and eloquent productions, to elevate, instruct, and refine the minds of his countrymen? Finally, has any one been more distinguished by exemplary fidelity in public office and by constant kindness and benevolence in private life? Few higher eulogies can be uttered than the reply which must rise to the lips of every one.

George Ticknor, Esq. then addressed the meeting as follows :—

Mr. President : I ask your permission to say a few words concerning the eminent associate and cherished friend whom we have lost,— so sadly, so suddenly lost. It is but little that I ·can say becoming the occasion, so well was he known of all ; for, in his early youth, he rose to a height, which has led us to watch and honor and understand, from the first, his long and brilliant career.

On looking back over the two centuries and a half of this our New England history, I recollect not more than three or four persons who, during as many years of a life protracted as his was beyond threescore and ten, have so much occupied the attention of the country,— I do not remember a single one, who has presented himself under such various, distinct, and remarkable aspects to classes of our community so separate, thus commanding a degree of interest from each, whether scholars, theologians, or statesmen, which in the aggregate of its popular influence has become so extraordinary. For he has been, to a marvellous degree successful, in whatever he has touched. His whole way of life for above fifty years ·can now be traced back by the monuments which he erected with his own hand as he advanced; each seeming, at the time, to be sufficient for the reputation of one man. Few here are old enough to remember when the first of these graceful monuments rose before us; none of us I apprehend is so young, that he will survive the splendor of their long line. And, now that we have come to its end, and that it seems as if the whole air were filled with our sorrowful and proud recollections, as it is with the light at noonday, we feel with renewed force that we have known him as we have known very few men of our time. And this is true. How, then, can I say anything that shall be worthy of memory; still less anything that is fit for record?

When he was ten or eleven years of age and I was about three years older, his family came to live within a few doors of my father's house and subsequently removed to a contiguous estate. But, at this time, Mr. President, when the City of Boston, I suppose, was not one fifth as large as it is now, neighborhood implied kindly acquaintance. I soon knew his elder brother, Alexander, then the leader of his class at Cambridge, while I was a student in a class one year later, at Dartmouth College. I at once conceived a strong admiration for that remarkable scholar;—an admiration, let me add, which has never been diminished since. The younger brother, of whom I saw little, was then in that humble school in Short Street which he has made classical by his occasional allusions to it, and to the two Websters who were his teachers there. From the elder of these, who was frequently at my father's house, I used to hear much about

the extraordinary talents and progress of this younger
Everett; praise which my admiration of his brother prevented me, I fear, from receiving, for a time, with so
glad a welcome as I ought to have done. During the
two or three subsequent years, while the younger brother
was at Exeter or beginning his career at Cambridge, I
knew little of him, though I was much with the elder
and belonged to at least one pleasant club of which he
was a member.

The first occasion on which the younger scholar's delightful character broke upon me, with its true attributes,
is still fresh in my recollection. It was in the summer of
1809. Mr. Alexander Everett was then about to embark
for St. Petersburg, as the private secretary of Mr. John
Quincy Adams, and a few nights before he left us, he
gave a supper—saddened, indeed, by the parting that was
so soon to follow, but still a most agreeable supper—to
eight or ten of his personal friends, one of whom [Dr.
Bigelow] I now see before me;—the last, except myself,
remaining of that well remembered symposium. The
younger brother was there, so full of gayety—unassum-
ing but irrepressible—so full of whatever is attractive in
manner or in conversation, that I was perfectly carried
captive by his light and graceful humor. And this, let
me here say, has always been a true element of his character. He was never at any period of his life a saturnine
man. In his youth he overflowed with animal spirits;
and, although from the time of his entrance into political
life, with the grave cares and duties that were imposed
upon him, the lightheartedness of his nature was some-

what oppressed or obscured, it was always there.   There
was never a time I think — excepting in those days of
trial and sorrow that come to all — in which, among the
private friends with whom he was most intimate, he was
not cheerful, nay charmingly amusing.   It was so the
very day before his death.   He was suffering from an
oppression on the lungs; and, as I sat with him, he
could speak only in whispers; but, even then, his natural
playfulness was not wanting.

But from the time of that delightful supper in 1809,
my regard never failed to be fastened on him.   At first,
during his under-graduate's life, at Cambridge, I saw him
seldom.   But in that simpler stage of our society, when
the interests of men were so different from what they
have become since, all who concerned themselves about
letters, were familiar with what was done and doing in
Cambridge.   Everett, youthful as he was, was eminently
the first scholar there, and we all knew it.   We all — or,
at least, all of us who were young — read the " Harvard
Lyceum," which he edited, and which, I may almost say,
he filled with his scholarship and humor.

In 1811 he was graduated with the highest honors,
and pronounced, with extraordinary grace of manner, a
short oration, on — if I rightly remember — " The Difficulties attending a Life of Letters," which delighted a
crowded audience, attracted more than was usual by the
expectations that waited on what is called " The first
part."   But thus far, what was most known of his life
was strictly academic, and was only more widely spread
than an academic reputation is wont to be because he

was himself already so full of recognized promise and power. His time, in fact, was not yet come. But the next year it came. He was invited to deliver the customary poem at Commencement, before the " Phi Beta Kappa Society." It was not, perhaps, a period, when much success could have been anticipated for anybody, on a merely literary occasion. The war with England had been declared only a few weeks earlier and men felt gloomy and disheartened at the prospect before them. Still more recently Buckminster had died, only twenty-eight years old, but loved and admired, as few men ever have been in this community; — mourned, too, as a loss to the beginnings of true scholarship among us, which many a scholar then thought might hardly be repaired. But, as in all cases of a general stir in the popular feeling, there was an excitement abroad which permitted the minds of men to be turned and wielded in directions widely different from that of the prevailing current. The difficulty was to satisfy the demands in such a disturbed condition of things. ·

Mr. Everett was then just in that " opening manhood " which Homer, with his unerring truth, has called " the fairest term of life." And how handsome he was, Mr. President! We all know how remarkable was Milton's early beauty. An engraving of him — a fine one — by Vertue, from a portrait preserved in the Onslow family, and painted when the poet was about twenty, is well known. But, sir, so striking was the resemblance of this engraving to our young friend, that I remember often seeing a copy of it inscribed with his name in capital letters, and am unable to say that the inscription was amiss. Radiant, then, with such personal attractions, he rose before an audience already disposed to receive him with extraordinary kindness.

His subject was, " American Poets," certainly not a very promising one. Of course his treatment of it was essentially didactic; but there was such a mixture of good-natured satire in it, so much more praise willingly accorded than was really deserved, such humorous and happy allusions to what was local, personal, and familiar to all, and such solemn and tender passages about the condition of our society, and its anxieties and losses, — that it was received with an applause which, in some respects, I have never known equalled. Graver and grander success I have often known to be achieved, on greater occasions, not only by others but by himself. But never did I witness such clear, unmingled delight. Everything was forgotten but the speaker and what he chose we should remember.

This success, it should be recollected, was gained when Mr. Everett was only a little more than eighteen years old. But, sir, in fact, it had been gained earlier. The poem had been read when he was only about seventeen, before a club of college friends in the latter part of his senior year, and had now been fitted by a few additions, for its final destination. Its publication was immediately demanded and urged. But on the whole it was determined not to give it fully to the world. Four copies, however, were privately struck off on large paper, one of which I received at the time from the author, and thirty-

22

six more in common octavo, which were at once dis-
tributed to other eager friends.   But this was by no means
enough.   A little later, therefore, there were printed,
with slight alterations, sixty copies more, of which he
gave me two, in an extra form, marked with his fair
autograph.   I know not where three others are now to
be found; though I trust, from the great contemporary
interest in the poem itself, and from its real value, that
many copies of it have been saved.

It is written in the versification consecrated by the
success of Dryden and Pope; and if it contains lines
marked by the characteristics of the early age at which it
was produced, there is yet a power in it, a richness of
thought, and a graceful finish, of which probably few men
at thirty would have been found capable.   At any rate, in
the hundred and more years during which verse had then
been printed in these Colonies and States, not two hundred
pages, I think, can now be found, which can be read
with equal interest and pleasure.

It was only a few weeks afterwards, as nearly as I
recollect, that he began to preach.   I heard his first two
sermons, delivered to a small congregation in a neighboring town, and I heard him often afterwards.   The effect
was always the same.   There was not only the attractive
manner, which we had already witnessed and admired,
but there was, besides, a devout tenderness, which had
hardly been foreseen.   The main result, however, had
been anticipated.   He was, in a few months, settled over
the church in Brattle Street, with the assent and admiration of all.

But, in the midst of his success in the pulpit, he was turned aside to become a controversial theologian. Early in the autumn of 1813, Mr. George B. English published a small book, entitled, " The Grounds of Christianity Examined by Comparing the New Testament with the Old." It was, in fact, an attack on the truth of the Christian religion, in the sense of Judaism. Its author, whom I knew personally, was a young man of very pleasant intercourse, and a great lover of books, of which he had read many, but with little order or well-defined purpose. He would, I think, have been a man of letters, if such a path had been open to him. A profession, however, was needful. He studied law, but became dissatisfied with it. He studied divinity, but was never easy in his course. His mind was never well balanced, or well settled upon anything. He was always an adventurer — just as much so in the scholarlike period of his life, as he was afterwards, when he served under Ismail Pasha, in Egypt, and attempted to revive the ancient war-chariots armed with scythes.

His ill-constructed book received several answers, direct and indirect, from the pulpit and the press; but none of them was entirely satisfactory, because their authors had not frequented the strange by-paths of learning in which Mr. English had for some time been wandering with perverse preference. Mr. Everett, however, followed him everywhere with a careful scholarship and exact logic unknown to his presumptuous adversary. His " Defence of Christianity " was published in 1814, and I still possess one, out of half a dozen copies of it that were printed for the author's friends, on extra paper, and are become curious as showing how ill understood, in those simpler days, were the dainty luxuries of bibliography. But the proper end of the book was quickly attained. Mr. English's imperfect and unsound learning was demolished at a blow; and, as has just been so happily said by Dr. Lothrop, the whole controversy, even Mr. Everett's part of it, is forgotten, because it has been impossible to keep up any considerable interest in a question which he had so absolutely settled. Mr. Everett's " Defence," however, will always remain a remarkable book. Some years after its publication, Professor Monk, of Cambridge, the biographer of Bentley, and himself afterwards Bishop of Gloucester, told me that he did not think any Episcopal library in England could be accounted complete which did not possess a copy of it.

In the winter following the publication of this book — that is, in the winter of 1814–15 — he was elected Professor of Greek Literature. I was then at the South, having made up my mind to pass some time at the University of Göttingen, and was endeavoring, chiefly among the Germans in the interior of Pennsylvania, to obtain information concerning the modes of teaching in Germany, about which there then prevailed in New England an absolute ignorance now hardly to be conceived. With equal surprise and delight, I received letters from my friend telling me of his appointment, and that, to qualify himself for the place offered him, he should endeavor to go with me upon what we both regarded as a sort of adventure, to Germany. Perhaps I should add that this sudden change in his course of life excited no small comment at the time, and that, especially by a part of the parish whose brilliant anticipations he thus disappointed, it was not accepted in a kindly spirit. But of its wisdom and rightfulness there was soon no doubt in the mind of anybody.

We embarked in April, 1815, and passed a few weeks in London, during the exciting period of Bonaparte's last campaign, and just at the time of the battle of Waterloo. But we were in a hurry to be at work. We hastened, therefore, through Holland, stopping chiefly to buy books, and early in August were already in the chosen place of our destination. It was our purpose to remain there a year. But the facilities for study were such as we had never heard or dreamt of. My own residence was in consequence protracted to a year and nine months, and Mr. Everett's was protracted yet six months longer — both of us leaving the tempting school at last sorry and unsatisfied.

How well he employed his time there the great results shown in his whole subsequent life have enabled the world to judge. I witnessed the process from day to day. We were constantly together. Except for the first few months, when we could not make convenient arrangements for it, we lived in contiguous rooms in the same house — the house of Bouterwek, the literary historian, and a favorite teacher in the university. During the vacations — except one, when he went to the Hague, to see his brother Alexander, then our Secretary of Legation in Holland — we travelled together about Germany; and

every day in term time we went more or less to the same
private teachers, and the same lecturers. But he struck
in his studies much more widely than I did. To say
nothing of his constant, indefatigable labor upon the
Greek with Dissen, he occupied himself a good deal with
Arabic under Eichhorn, he attended lectures upon modern
history by Heeren, and upon the civil law by Hugo, and
he followed besides the courses of other professors, whose
teachings I did not frequent and whose names I no longer
remember.

His power of labor was prodigious; unequalled in my
experience. One instance of it — the more striking, perhaps, because disconnected from his regular studies — is,
I think, worth especial notice. We had been in Göttingen, I believe, above a year, and he was desirous to send
home something of what he had learnt about the modes
of teaching, not only there, but in our visits to the universities of Leipzig, Halle, Jena, and Berlin, and to the great
preparatory schools of Meissen, and Pfrote. He had, as
nearly as I can recollect, just begun this task. But how
so voluminous a matter was to be sent home was an
important question. Regular packets there were none,
even between New York and Liverpool. We depended,
therefore, very much on accident — altogether on tran-
sient vessels. Opportunities from Hamburg were rare
and greatly valued. Just at this time our kind mercantile correspondents at that port gave us sudden notice
that a vessel for Boston would sail immediately. There
was not a moment to be lost; Mr. Everett threw everything else aside, and worked for thirty-five consecutive

hours on his letter, despatching it as the mail was closing. But, though sadly exhausted by his labor, he was really uninjured, and in a day or two was fully refreshed and restored. I need not say that a man who did this was in earnest in what he undertook. But let me add, Mr. President, that, by the constant, daily exercise of dispositions and powers like these, he laid during those two or three years in Göttingen, the real foundations on which his great subsequent success, in so many widely different ways, safely rested. I feel as sure of this as I do of any fact of the sort within my knowledge.

When I left Göttingen, he and a young American friend [Stephen H. Perkins]— then under his charge, and who still survives — accompanied me on my first day's journey. At Hesse Cassel we separated, thinking to meet again in the south of Europe, and visit together Greece and Asia Minor, which, from the time of the appearance of " Childe Harold," four or five years earlier, had been much in our young thoughts and imaginations. But " Forth rushed the Lévant and the Ponent winds." A few months afterwards, at Paris, I received the appointment of Professor of French and Spanish Literature, at Cambridge; and, from that moment, it was as plain that my destination was Madrid, as it was that he was bound to go to Athens and Constantinople. We did not, therefore, meet again until his return home, in the autumn of 1819, where I had preceded him by a few months.

From this time Mr. Everett's life has been almost constantly a public one, and all have been able to judge him freely and fully. He began his lectures on Greek literature at Cambridge the next summer, and I went from Boston regularly to hear them, for the pleasure and instruction they gave me. The notes I then took of them, and which I still preserve, will bear witness to the merit just ascribed to them by the friend on my left, who heard the same course somewhat later.

But Mr. Everett was, in another sense, already a public man. From the natural concern he felt in the fate of a country he had so recently visited, he took a great interest, as early as 1821–23, in the Greek Revolution, and wrote and spoke on it, both as a philanthropic and as a political question. In 1824 he was elected to Congress. There and elsewhere, like other public men of eminence, he has had his political trials and his political opponents; sometimes generous, sometimes unworthy, but never touching the unspotted purity of his character and purposes. All such discussions, however, find no becoming place within these doors. We recognize here no such divisions of opinion respecting our lamented associate. We remember his great talents, and the gentleness that added to their power; his extraordinary scholarship, and the rich fruits it bore; his manifold public services, and the just honors that have followed them. All this we remember. In all of it we rejoice. We recollect, too, that for five-and-forty years, he has been our pride and ornament, as a member of this Society. But we recognize no external disturbing element in these our happy recollections. To us, he has always been the same. At any meeting that we have held since he became fully known to us and to the country, the beautiful, appropriate, and truthful resolutions now on your table, might — if he had just been taken from us as he has been now — have been passed by us with as much earnestness and unanimity, as they will be amidst our sorrow to-night. They do but fitly complete our record of what has always been true. And let us feel thankful, as we adopt this record and make it our own, that — grand and gratifying as it is — neither the next generation nor any that may follow will desire to have a word of it obliterated or altered.

Hon. John H. Clifford then proceeded as follows :—

MR. PRESIDENT: Having been unable to participate in the last offices of respect to the remains of our departed associate, and feeling obliged to decline the distinguished service to which I was invited, of pronouncing a more elaborate address upon his life and character before the two Houses of the Legislature, I could not forego the opportunity of uniting in this office of commemoration, with an Association in which he took so generous an interest, and of which he was so eminent a member.

However inadequate must be any expression of my sense of the loss we have sustained, I cannot doubt that the assurance of a simple, heartfelt tribute of personal affection and gratitude, when he was to be remembered in a circle like this, would have been more grateful to *him* than any studied words of eulogy, though they were polished into a rhetoric as brilliant as his own.

It is thus only, that I desire to speak of him — my honored chief, my wise and trusted counsellor — my ever constant friend. It was from his hands that I received,

23

now just thirty years ago, my first commission in the service of the State; and from that period up to the close of the last month of the last year, he honored me with a correspondence which I have carefully preserved as a precious possession for myself and for my children. You will pardon me, Mr. President, if, in this brief review of what I owe to the influence of his friendship and his counsels, I shall invoke his presence, still to speak to us, by a free and unreserved reference to this correspondence.

Admitted to the intimate intercourse of a member of his military family, during the entire term of his service as Governor of the Commonwealth, he never afterwards ceased to manifest the interest in me which that intercourse implied, and the value of which no poor words of mine, of public or of private acknowledgment can ever measure or repay. Of that military family, Mr. President,— and " we were seven,"— who bore his commission during those four years of brilliant service to his native Commonwealth, you and I are the only survivors, to render these last honors to our illustrious chief.

In the review of his remarkable career, to which, since its triumphant close on earth, the minds of so many have been turned who never knew him otherwise than in his public character, I am persuaded that some impressions respecting him, which those who were brought nearest to him know to be utterly unfounded, are certain to be corrected when the materials of a just judgment of all that he was, and all that he did, are open to the examination of his countrymen.

It has been said of him that he was of a cold and unsympathizing nature. There never was a more mistaken judgment of any public man than this. If he possessed any trait more distinctly marked than another, it was his unfaltering fidelity to his friends, and his warm and generous interest in everything that touched their happiness and welfare, as well in the trials and the sorrows, as in the successes and the sunshine of life.

While he was representing the country with such signal ability at the Court of St. James, and in the midst of the grave and perplexing questions which he there discussed and disposed of with such masterly skill, I had occasion to communicate to him the death of a much loved child, in whom he had taken great interest, and who bore his name. In a letter written on the receipt of the intelligence, and under circumstances that might well have excused him from an immediate reply,— and which would have excused him, if that reply had been prompted by anything less than a sincere and unaffected sympathy, which does not belong to a cold and formal nature,— he says: " I was staying at Sir Robert Peel's, with a very agreeable party, consisting of several of the cabinet ministers, and my diplomatic brethren, when I received your letter, which has cast a shade of sadness over my visit that I feel as little inclination as ability to throw off. . . . . . But let us not speak of our beloved ones as taken from us. They are, in truth, not lost, but gone before. They have accomplished, in the dawn of life, the work which grows harder, the longer the time that is given us to do it."

Equally erroneous, in my judgment, is the opinion that Mr. Everett, as a public man, was lacking in moral courage. There were occasions in his life when it would have required less courage, and have cost a smaller sacrifice to escape this imputation, and secure to himself the popular favor, than it did to invite it. But his resolute adherence to his own conscientious convictions, his large and comprehensive patriotism, his unswerving nationality and love of the Union, and the knowledge which a scholar's studies and a statesman's observations had given him of the perils by which that Union was environed, closed many an avenue of popularity to him, which bolder, but *not* more courageous, public men than he could consent to walk in.

If timidity consists in an absence of all temerity and rashness, of entire freedom from that reckless spirit which so often leads " fools to rush in where angels fear to tread," let it be ever remembered to his honor, that Mr. Everett was a timid statesman. But if the virtue of moderation is still to be counted among the excellent qualities of a ruler or counsellor, in conducting the complex and delicate questions of policy which affect the well-being of a country like ours, and which bear upon its future fortunes as well as its present favor, let it also be remembered that our departed statesman, while he adhered inflexibly to his convictions of the right, was not " ashamed to let his moderation be known unto all men."

In this aspect of his character, it has seemed to me that

the great Pater Patriæ, whom he had so diligently studied, and his oration upon whom wrought as great a work upon his countrymen as his unsurpassed biographical sketch of him in the " Encyclopædia Britannica" has had upon the foreign estimate of Washington, was " his great example, as he was his theme."

It has been not an unfrequent criticism upon Mr. Everett's career, that it was in a certain sense a failure, because, with his scholarly tastes, his patient industry, his affluent learning and his great opportunities, he would leave behind him no " great work" as the fruit of all his accomplishments and powers. If it be a worthy ambition in one of great endowments and liberal culture, to do the greatest good to the greatest number of his fellow-men, and to make the world better for his having lived in it, this is a mistaken criticism. It is true his resources were ample to have accomplished any " great work," such as this criticism implies, in any of the fields of intellectual activity, from which great scholars gather their ripened harvests. He could have graced the shelves of our libraries with precious octavos of history, or science, or literature. But to have done this he would have foregone that " greater work" which he did accomplish, and of which the three volumes already published, to be followed we trust by many more, will stand forever as the witness and the memorial — " *Non omnia omnes possumus.*" And he appointed to himself the nobler task of elevating the public taste, — of bringing before a working people the highest truths of philosophy in a style of adaptation to their wants before unknown — of diffusing throughout the community a knowledge of great historical events and their application to the duties of living men, — of implanting in the breasts of the people a reverence for their God-fearing ancestors, and in justifying the ways of Providence to them and their posterity, — of displaying before them the brightest deeds and the most heroic sacrifices of patriotism, and thereby inspiring in them the warmest love of their country, and instructing them in the duties they owed to her, — all these, and more, of the glorious proofs that his life was a noble success and in no sense a failure, glow in every page of his writings, not one of which in dying would he need to blot, from that first lecture before the Mechanics' Institute in Charlestown, down to that last fervid, Christian appeal in Faneuil Hall.

Mr. President, I speak in the faith of the clearest conviction, that whatever of unjust, or censorious, or honestly mistaken judgment, has ever been passed upon our departed friend, will be surely modified, if not entirely reversed, in all candid minds, under the lights with which a true and complete history of his life will illuminate it, from its earliest promise to its latest most glorious record. Already one of his contemporaries, who has made his own name " imperishable in immortal song," in words of manly confession, as honorable to their author as they are just to the memory of him of whom they were spoken, has anticipated the verdict of history.

" If," says Mr. Bryant, " I have uttered anything in derogation of Mr. Everett's public character at times when it seemed to me that he did not resist with becoming spirit the aggressions of wrong, I now, looking back upon his noble record of the last four years, retract it at his grave, — I lay upon his hearse the declaration of my sorrow that I saw not then the depth of his worth, — that I did not discern under the conservatism that formed a part of his nature, that generous courage which a great emergency could so nobly awaken."

But the praises of men were now of little worth, had we not one source of pride and affection open to us in the contemplation of this beneficent life, the value of which no words of eulogy, apt as they are to run into exaggeration, can express too strongly. The manifold temptations of public life, whether insinuating themselves through our domestic politics, or the social and political ethics of the national capitol, in the arts of diplomacy or through the enervating allurements of foreign courts, which in some of their Protean forms are so apt to assail the home-taught virtue of our public men, never left a trace of their influence upon the purity of his unsullied character. To those who had the closest view of him, there was always apparent his constant recognition of the presence and direction of a Higher Power in all the concerns of life. Abundant illustrations of this, indeed, may be found in his published works. Who that has read it, who especially that had your privilege and mine, Mr. President, of listening to it as it fell from his lips, can have forgotten that magnificent passage, in my judgment the most eloquent he ever uttered, in his speech at the centennial celebration at Barnstable in 1839? — a passage which the late Chief Justice Shaw, who was present, declared to me was, in his opinion, unsurpassed in modern history.

After describing the condition of " the Mayflower freighted with the destinies of a continent, as she crept almost sinking into Provincetown harbor, utterly incapable of living through another gale, approaching the shore precisely where the broad sweep of this remarkable headland presents almost the only point at which for hundreds of miles she could with any ease have made a harbor," he adds: " I feel my spirit raised above the sphere of mere natural agencies. I see the mountains of New England rising from their rocky thrones. They rush forward into the ocean, settling down as they advance; and there they range themselves, a mighty bulwark around the heaven-directed vessel. Yes, the everlasting God himself stretches out the arm of his mercy and his power in substantial manifestations, and gathers the meek company of his worshippers as in the hollow of his hand."

But a more striking, because a more spontaneous expression of the same characteristic spirit, is contained in a letter of farewell which I received from him, dated at New York on the day before his embarkation for Europe with his whole family in the summer of 1840, and of course written amidst all the distractions incident to the preparations for his voyage.

The intelligence of the burning of the packet ship Poland at sea, and the rescue of her passengers from imminent peril by a passing vessel, had then just been received in this country. " The fate of the Poland," he writes, " makes me feel strongly how near to death we are in the midst of life. I embark with all my treasures

with some misgivings. But having undertaken the voyage
from proper motives, I seem to be in the path of duty,
and I am sure I am in the hand of God.   There are many
paths to his presence.   And whether they lead us singly,
or in families, or companies, — whether by a bed of lan-
guishing on land, or the blazing deck of a burning vessel,
or the dark abyss of the sea, can be of but little consequence in the existence of an undying spirit."

When his own hour had come, Mr. President, it was
through no such avenue of suspense and sufferings as
these that his Heavenly Father took him to himself.   But
in welcoming him, as our faith assures us, to the rewards
of a " good and faithful servant," He bore him from our
sight so graciously as to leave us nothing to regret from
him, either in his death or in his life.   Why should we
mourn over such a death, — the serene close of such a life
on earth, the entrance upon the assured rewards of the
Life Eternal ?

> " If ever lot was prosperously cast,
>   If ever life was like the lengthened flow
>   Of some sweet music, sweetness to the last,
>   'T was his." . . . .

Not the music of that matchless voice alone, whose
inspiring cadences seem still to linger in our ears, as we
assemble in this room, where it so often charmed and
instructed us, but the diviner harmony to which he gave
such magnificent expression by a rounded and completed
life, — a life that was mercifully spared to his country for
its greatest work during its closing years ; whose music,

24

during those years of a nation's regeneration, was but a prolongation of the music of the Union, by which he marched, himself, and inspired his countrymen to march, to the great conflict with treason and with wrong.

Here, and wherever throughout the world, in all coming time, the gospel of constitutional liberty is preached among men, shall this, his last, greatest work, " be told as a memorial of him." One word more, Mr. President, and my grateful task is done.

In the correspondence from which I have so freely quoted, I found, a day or two ago, a striking passage, which seems to me a fitting close for this feeble tribute to the memory of a loved and honored friend. In a letter written to me from Washington early in 1854, the year that he resigned his place in the Senate of the United States, he says: "I have never filled an office which I did not quit more cheerfully than I entered. I am not sure that it is not so in most cases with the last great act of retirement, not from the offices and duties of life, but from life itself."

Brethren, to what far-off sphere of celestial fruition may we not, without presumption, in that spirit of faith which he so strongly cherished, follow our departed associate, and hear again the music of that voice, repeating this sentiment, now verified and made certain in the supreme experience of that last Sabbath morning?

Dr. Walker spoke as follows : —

Mr. PRESIDENT: Leaving it for others to speak of Mr. Everett's eminence as a scholar and as a statesman, and of the purity and beauty of his daily life, I ask permission to say a few words of his administration as President of Harvard College. There is, I believe, a prevailing impression in the community, that this part of his public career was less successful than the rest. If so, it is to be imputed, in no small measure, to three causes which have hindered his merits and services as Head of the University from being duly appreciated.

The first of these causes was his known distaste for the office. Most of us remember, that when he was appointed to the place, the community were of one mind as to his being precisely the man to fill it, — with a single exception; but that was an important exception, for it was *himself*. This distaste was never entirely overcome; and there are those who have construed it into evidence of want of success. They might have done so with some show of reason, if it had grown up in the office; for, in that case, it might be regarded as resulting, at least in some degree, from disappointed hopes. But when it is considered that the distaste was as strong, and perhaps stronger, when he accepted the office, than when he laid it down, there would seem to be no ground for such a construction.

The second cause which has hindered the public from duly appreciating Mr. Everett's services to the College as President, is found in the nature of the reforms and improvements attempted and actually introduced by him. With his accustomed method and thoroughness, he could not do otherwise than begin at the beginning. Accordingly, one of his first undertakings was to prepare and publish, under the proper authorities, a careful revision of the college laws. This was a most important and necessary work, which cost months of anxious labor; yet not likely to attract public attention, nor even to be known beyond the precincts of the University. Again, he believed that all improvements in the college, to be of much solidity, must have their foundation in its improved moral and religious condition. No president ever labored more assiduously or more anxiously for this end, nor, considering the time occupied, with more success. Indeed, I cannot help thinking that it is for the measures he instituted or suggested with a view to promote the moral elevation of the college, that its friends have most reason to hold him in grateful remembrance. Yet these also were matters which, from their very nature, did not admit of display, and some of them not even of publicity; nay more, in the beginning they were not unlikely to occasion some degree of opposition and trouble.

But the principal cause hindering a due appreciation of Mr. Everett's presidency of the college, brief as it was, is doubtless this very brevity. If his health had permitted him to retain the office ten years, I have no doubt that many things which were offensive to him would have disappeared. His attention, meanwhile, would have been turned to proper academical reforms, noticeable in themselves, and bringing the college into notice by extending its influence and fame. And this, together with the just pride taken in his distinguished name, and the unsurpassed dignity with which he represented the University on all public occasions, would have made his administration forever illustrious in the annals of the college; and even, within its limited scope, as illustrious *for him* as any other part of his public career. Nor is this all. It would then have been seen that the first four years, those which we really had, were an appropriate and necessary introduction to the whole; and as such, *they* would have come in for their full share of the glory.

Dr. Holmes read the following Poem: —

OUR FIRST CITIZEN.

WINTER'S cold drift lies glistening o'er his breast;
    For him no spring shall bid the leaf unfold;
What Love could speak, by sudden grief oppressed,
    What swiftly summoned Memory tell, is told.

Even as the bells, in one consenting chime,
    Filled with their sweet vibrations all the air,
So joined all voices, in that mournful time,
    His genius, wisdom, virtues, to declare.

What place is left for words of measured praise,
    Till calm-eyed History, with her iron pen,
Grooves in the unchanging rock the final phrase
    That shapes his image in the souls of men?

Yet while the echoes still repeat his name,
    While countless tongues his full-orbed life rehearse,
Love, by his beating pulses taught, will claim
    The breath of song, the tuneful throb of verse,—

Verse that, in ever-changing ebb and flow,
  Moves, like the laboring heart, with rush and rest,
Or swings in solemn cadence, sad and slow,
  Like the tired heaving of a grief-worn breast.

This was a mind so rounded, so complete, —
  No partial gift of Nature in excess, —
That, like a single stream where many meet,
  Each separate talent counted something less.

A little hillock, if it lonely stand,
  Holds o'er the fields an undisputed reign,
While the broad summit of the table-land
  Seems with its belt of clouds a level plain.

Servant of all his powers, that faithful slave,
  Unsleeping Memory, strengthening with his toils,
To every ruder task his shoulder gave,
  And loaded every day with golden spoils.

Order, the law of Heaven, was throned supreme
  O'er action, instinct, impulse, feeling, thought;
True as the dial's shadow to the beam,
  Each hour was equal to the charge it brought.

Too large his compass for the nicer skill
  That weighs the world of science grain by grain;
All realms of knowledge owned the mastering will
  That claimed the franchise of his whole domain.

Earth, air, sea, sky, the elemental fire,
  Art, history, song, — what meanings lie in each
Found in his cunning hand a stringless lyre,
  And poured their mingling music through his speech.

Thence flowed those anthems of our festal days,
   Whose ravishing division held apart
The lips of listening throngs in sweet amaze,
   Moved in all breasts the self-same human heart.

Subdued his accents, as of one who tries
   To press some care, some haunting sadness down;
His smile half shadow; and to stranger eyes
   The kingly forehead wore an iron crown.

He was not armed to wrestle with the storm,
   To fight for homely truth with vulgar power;
Grace looked from every feature, shaped his form, —
   The rose of Academe, — the perfect flower!

Such was the stately scholar whom we knew
   In those ill days of soul-enslaving calm,
Before the blast of Northern vengeance blew
   Her snow-wreathed pine against the Southern palm.

Ah, God forgive us! did we hold too cheap
   The heart we might have known, but would not see,
And look to find the nation's friend asleep
   Though the dread hour of her Gethsemane?

That wrong is past; we gave him up to Death
   With all a hero's honors round his name;
As martyrs coin their blood, he coined his breath,
   And dimmed the scholar's in the patriot's fame.

So shall we blazon on the shaft we raise, —
   Telling our grief, our pride, to unborn years, —
" He who had lived the mark of all men's praise
   Died with the tribute of a nation's tears."

The Hon. Richard H. Dana then spoke as follows : —

Mr. President : This full tide of grief and admiration has carried along with it all there is of eulogy, and there seems nothing left for me to-night — not wishing to say over what has been so well said — but a single, common-place suggestion, exciting no feeling, and entirely below the demands of the hour. I would simply remind you, brethren, that the fame of Mr. Everett has been fairly earned.

It seems to me that he has earned his fame as fairly as the painter, the poet, the sculptor, and the composer earn theirs. The artist submits his picture or statue, the composer his oratorio, and the poet his epic or lyric to the judgment of time, and abides the result. Mr. Everett, for fifty years, year by year, submitted to the judgment of his age orations, essays, lectures, speeches, and diplomatic letters, and abided the result. If the judgment has been favorable to him, what can have been more fairly earned?

It has not only been earned without fraud on the public judgment, or mistake or accident, but it has been earned in strict compliance with the primeval law of labor — that in the sweat of the brow all bread shall be eaten. It has not been the result of a few happy strokes of genius. He never did anything except with all the might his mind and body could lend to it. He was first scholar at Har-vard, because four years of competition left him so. If he was in anything more learned than other men, it was because he did his best with great natural powers. No occasions occurred to him that may not occur to all. What other men made little of, he made everything of. He never trusted to genius or to chance. He owes as little, too, as any man, to the posts he has filled. Many derive importance from holding offices that connect them with great events. He stands upon his work, irrespective of office; and, indeed, his best and brightest acts have been those of a private citizen. Yes, brethren, every stone in the monument he has builded to himself has been quarried, fashioned, and polished by his own hand and eye.

Fairly earned, his fame is also firmly fixed. His style of thought and expression in written address has been tried by the tests of novelty and of familiarity, of sameness and of variety, in old communities and in new communities; and that style which forty years before, in its freshness, charmed the choice spirits of a critical community of readers and scholars, was found in its maturity, nay, almost in its age, equal to the conflict with the trained diplomatists of Europe, before the forum of nations.

So of his elocution. An orator may, by accidental charm of voice or manner, or by tricks of speech, gain celebrity for a time; but the crucial test comes, and he is found wanting, or he palls and stales by mere custom. But Mr. Everett's style of speech has been tried by every test, applied to every variety of topic, in different countries, and has survived the changes and chances of taste and opinion, as potent with the sons and daughters as with their fathers and mothers. At threescore and ten the spell of his elocution was as effective as in the freshness of his youth or the vigor of his manhood. The eloquence which forty and fifty years ago filled Brattle Street Church to the window-tops, which, in its new-born beauty, charmed the select assemblages at Cambridge, Concord, and Plymouth, was found in its gray and bent age, equal — more equal than any other — to the exigencies and shocks of the most vast and momentous popular canvass the world ever knew.

The Hon. B. F. Thomas spoke as follows : —

MR. PRESIDENT: If I had consulted my own judgment only, it would have been to listen to the gentlemen around me, the early, the life-long companions of the illustrious dead. I may not claim to have been of Mr. Everett's intimate friends. Though I have met him occasionally in private life, my means of knowledge are, after all, those of a reader and hearer of his public discourse. Nor have I, during a portion of his public life, been drawn to him by ties of political affinity and sympathy. Possibly, following the courtesies of parliamentary assemblies, these considerations may have led to the request that I should say a word this evening.

If the object of these services of commemoration were indiscriminate eulogy, the custom were more honored in the breach than in the observance; such service being good neither for the dead nor the living. If we had no higher or nobler purpose, we might well turn to the pressing duties of life and of the hour, and let the dead bury their dead.

But if we believe the saying of an old historian, cited by Bolingbroke, that history is philosophy teaching by examples; if, rejecting the godless speculations of Buckle, we recognize in history the power and influence of the individual spirit; if we see in the lives of great and good men not only beacon lights on the line of human progress, but the most efficient of motive powers, the *causæ causantes;* that great and good men not only make history, but constitute history, and the best part of history; no work can be more appropriate to an historical society than the commemoration of such a life.

As you well observed, Mr. President, the other day in Faneuil Hall, in a speech, let me say, so worthy of its theme, one knows hardly where to begin or where to end. If we had but one word to say, it would be perhaps that Mr. Everett was the most *accomplished* man our country had produced; of the widest, most varied and finished culture. That using the word " orator," in the sense in which it has come to us from classic times, he was our most finished " orator," in fertility of resources, in aptness of use in grace of manner, in compass and music of voice, in curious felicity of diction, seldom if ever surpassed. Not always evincing magnetic power or projectile force, or the *ars artium celare artem;* but in his best and happiest moods recalling the lines in which Milton, with such marvellous beauty, has described Adam, wrapt, entranced with the last accents that fell from the lips of Raphael: —

> "The angel ended; but in Adam's ear
> So charming left his voice that he awhile
> Thought him still speaking — still stood fixed to hear."

Though it was as a graceful and eloquent orator that Mr. Everett was most widely known to his day and generation, we feel that in saying this we have not got very near to our subject; that we have not touched upon the lines of character which make the life of a great or good man the worthy subject of study and contemplation.

Outside of revelation, Mr. President, men make their own gods. They project them from within. They clothe them with their own passions, they dwarf them by their own infirmities. So it is in the construction of our heroes and great men. We not only admire chiefly the qualities in which we discover some resemblance to our own; but we are very apt to dwell on them as the salient points of character. We insist upon casting men into the moulds of our own minds. This may be natural, but it is neither manly nor just. That only is a manly and catholic criticism which appreciates and admires qualities utterly diverse from our own; which recollects that our antipodes stand also on the solid earth; that there may be diversities of gifts but the same spirit, differences of administration but the same Lord; that the eye cannot say to the hand, I have no need of thee, nor the head to the feet, I have no need of you; that this diversity of gifts and tendencies is part of God's economy for the well-being and progress of the race.

It is by the conflict and balance of forces that the planets know their places and " each in his motion like an angel sings." A like conflict and balance of forces is the law of human life and progress. In the shallow philosophy of Pope, there is not a shallower commonplace, than

" Just as the twig is bent the tree's inclined." You may twist and distort the growth of the tree, you may prune it into fantastic shapes, but the tree as God meant it to be lies wrapt in the germ, before the warm embrace of earth sends it up to greet the sun. The natural differences of men overcome and outgrow all culture and discipline. These two sons of the same parents, bred at the same fireside, trained in the same schools, surrounded by the same influences, ripened into manhood, the one shall become in politics a radical, the other a conservative. In religion one shall be the most protesting of protestants, the other repose with a child's trust on the bosom of the church.

In all free governments political parties are formed, and though they spring up sometimes for local and temporary purposes, yet as a general fact and in their last analysis, they will be found to be radical and conservative, the one having progress as its constant aim, the other dwelling upon the limitations of progress.

In the best sense of the word Mr. Everett was a conservative. No man more thoroughly understood or more fully appreciated the free institutions which the toils and sacrifices of good and wise and true men of twenty generations had secured to us. He had faith that whatever of error and imperfection was to be found in the work of the fathers would be removed by peaceful methods, by the progress of science, and art, and Christian culture and civilization. With his conservatism was found a broad, liberal, and catholic spirit. Bred in the extreme school of Protestantism, he did not understand by liberal Christianity the negation of things divine, the bowing of religion out of the circle of the human mind. He did not exclude from his idea of mental liberty the " liberty of obedience ; " the liberty with which Christ makes men free.

Bred in the school of the Puritans, illustrating their virtues, admiring their sublime devotion to duty, he could not have loved Puritanism the less because it was associated with the venerable past, because time had softened and hallowed its more rugged features, because distance lent enchantment to the view.

Bred in a school of politics, which, though of the highest integrity, had strong sectional tendencies, he was among the most national of our statesmen. No part of the land was shut out from his sympathy and regard. His patriotism covered the country, however bounded. No word dropped from his lips or pen to promote sectional hate or strife. His public life was a ministry of concord and peace. He understood the compromises of the Constitution, and was ready faithfully to abide by them. He appreciated and admired this marvellous frame of government, by which, for the first time in history, central power was reconciled with local independence, the immunities of free States with the capacities of a great empire. From the first to the last, through evil report and through good report, he clung to the Union of these States and to the Constitution as its only bond. No man labored more earnestly and devotedly to avert the coming strife. His dread of civil conflict seemed to wear at times almost the aspect of timidity. But if he felt more strongly it was because he foresaw more clearly.

No greater injustice can be done to Mr. Everett, than by the suggestion that in the last three or four years of his life his opinions had undergone a radical change, and that the services of the past three years were a sort of propitiation and atonement for those that had gone before. Some of the views of public policy developed by Mr. Everett within the last two years did not command my assent. That was equally true with some of his earlier opinions. But I can see no necessary conflict between Mr. Everett the conservative statesman, the life-long defender of the Union and the Constitution, and Mr. Everett the ardent supporter of a war to secure from destruction that Union and Constitution. Difference of judgment as to what might be effected by force of arms might be the result of changes in the condition of the country, in the unity of sentiment and action in the loyal States. What seemed to him impossible in 1861, might, from the success of our arms, seem feasible in 1864. So measures that he deemed to be impolitic at the first period might seem to him to be demanded by the necessities of the second. Those differences marked no radical change of principles; and one, who differed from him on some few questions of policy while adhering to his general views, may be pardoned a word to save him from the too great kindness of his later friends.

Honor, as the heart shall prompt, his labors to uphold the arm of government against secession, to give unity to its counsels and efforts, to bring all men to its standard. We may honor none the less a life given to what his nephew and my friend has fitly called the ministry of

conciliation, to the victories of peace. Nor will we forget
how, at the first glimpse of opportunity, he turned to his
first love; how, when the cry of suffering came from a
conquered city, his heart went out to meet and to help it;
how naturally he recurred to the power of Christian sympathies and kindness; how the blessed words of the
royal preacher of Israel sprung to his lips, "If thine
enemy hunger, feed him; if he thirst, give him drink."

Blessed close of a great and good life. Blessed privilege to forget for a moment the horrors and glories even
of war, the shouts and waving banners of triumph, to sit
again at the feet of the Divine Master, to lean upon his
bosom, to be kindled by and to radiate his divine love.

Hon. James Savage made the following remarks : —

MR. PRESIDENT: I am a little surprised to be called up;
and yet, sir, as the catalogue of the Society shows, Mr.
Everett's name stood next to mine, I hope I may be excused if the infirmity of age is more apparent than anything else in what I say.   I can refer to the early days of
Mr. Everett, which has not been more than once alluded
to, and that before he had adopted the resolution of taking
the profession of a preacher of the Everlasting Gospel.
In this he was most eminently successful, and before that
I remember well, sir, that the boy was father to the man.

No one who then looked at him and heard him, would
have failed to foretell the success which attended him.   Of
Mr. Everett, I supposse it can be said as of other men,
that he touched nothing that he did not adorn.   I cannot

give you the Latin, sir, but it is one of the very strong illustrations of human grace and felicity. It was very observable. When I was in England I had the advantage of great attention from Mr. Everett. When their chief statesman, Sir Robert Peel, was suddenly stricken down by instant death — and when the Earl of Aberdeen, another great friend of our country, succeeded him, continuing to maintain all our just rights consistent with the rights of his own country, — I had the advantage of meeting at Mr. Everett's, more than once or twice, some of the first gentlemen of England, chiefly official persons, and there to observe that no man of their own country was more attended to or less inclined to presume upon that attention. He seemed to be always the servant of the public in private as well as in public. I believe that our country has never had a superior minister anywhere at any court. I only wish that our present representative, my younger friend, may make Mr. Everett's place good.

Hon. Emory Washburn addressed the meeting as follows : —

MR. PRESIDENT : I shall not presume, in such a presence, to speak of Mr. Everett as a scholar, for I should feel that, by so doing, I was trespassing upon ground which would be so much more properly occupied by others. Nor will the time allotted me, admit of my dwelling upon the prominent part which he has taken in the historic events of the last thirty years of his life.

On the other hand, I cannot pretend to that intimate relation in the associations with him with which I have been favored, which would justify my attempting to draw

26

the nicer shades of character which intimacy alone enables one to analyze and trace. The most I can hope to do, is to give, in general terms, the results upon my own mind of the observation of more than forty years, chiefly, of his public life. And yet I have too often shared in his acts of personal kindness and courtesy, not to feel that I have a right to speak, also, of some of those traits of private character which stand out so prominently in the history of his life.

The impression which my study and observation of Mr. Everett's career have left most strongly defined upon my own mind, is its harmony and completeness in all its parts and characteristic qualities. In no field of honor or usefulness which he was called upon to occupy, did he ever fail to meet its reasonable requirements, nor did he ever shrink from the labor which its duties imposed. Many men have been great in one department of intellectual power or excellence, without possessing any claims to distinction in any other. Some cultivate one set of their powers or faculties, at the expense of the others. And of many, the judgments which we form, are but the balancing of one quality against another, the good against the evil, in order to ascertain at what point in the scale of moral worth we are to place them, in the estimate which we form of their character. The great warrior may be the brutal tyrant or the sordid miser. The brilliant poet may not soar above the atmosphere of his own vices, and the splendid orator while arousing and wielding the passions of others, at his will, may be the veriest slave of his own. Examples like these serve to mark the contrast of good and evil which are found in so many of the men whom the world has called famous.

But in the life of Mr. Everett, we seek, in vain, for any such contrasts as these. It was not because there were not, in the constitution of his mind and character, prominent and striking qualities, but because there was no occasion to go through the process of balancing these qualities against each other, in order to determine the relative rank of merit in which he is hereafter to be held in the judgment of posterity. His character in this respect was homogeneous in its elements, and complete, as well in its parts, as in the relations of these to each other.

That which must have struck every one who knew Mr. Everett as worthy of special notice, was the *filling up*, if I may so say, which gave to his life and character that roundness of proportion which renders it difficult, as we now look upon it, to say which of the traits for which he was distinguished, stand out most prominently upon the canvas. The picture is therefore in danger of being indistinct, from the absence of shade by which to bring out its features into bolder relief. He was the scholar at the same time that he was the orator of the pulpit and of the senate. He was the statesman and the diplomatist, the administrative officer, and, for many years of his life, the leading citizen in all the land. He was the Christian gentleman and the patriot; — and he won in them all, the respect and admiration of the country. And yet, who is now ready to say in which of these he transcended his own excellence in any other trait into which his character may be divided? Had he been either of these alone, there would have been, in the graces and accomplishments which he would have brought to its duties, enough to have given to his life in that sphere, the seeming finish of completeness. This is what I mean by that filling up which gave such an admirable fulness and consistency of proportion, in his character and life.

I might illustrate this thought further by referring to what is familiar, perhaps, to us all. It is more than forty years since I first heard him in the pulpit. I need not say with how much delight I listened to the rich and varied thought, the beauty of diction, the inimitable power of description, the affluence of illustration, and the pathos of appeal which gave so much life to his sermons of that day. These qualities of high pulpit oratory may not have been peculiar to him. But there was added to these, a beauty of countenance, a grace in action, a sweetness in voice, and an impressive, though almost measured modulation in tone and cadence, which left upon the mind of the hearer the conviction that he was unsurpassed as a rhetorician and an orator.

I afterwards heard him on the floor of Congress, and there he was no less at home than in the pulpit. And the dignity of his bearing, the mastery he showed of his subject, and the eloquence of the language he uttered, commanded the willing attention of that body, while it was yet dignified by men of eloquence and a national fame.

We all know how faithfully and conscientiously he performed the duties of the Executive of this Commonwealth. Nothing was left undone which courtesy, or kindness, or etiquette, claimed at his hand, from patiently listening to the broken language of the wife or mother pleading for the pardon of a wayward husband or son, to those dignified state papers which came from his pen perfect in all their parts. The same may be said of the manner in which he bore himself at the court of St. James, and as successor of Mr. Webster, at the head of our American court at Washington.

And in this, I do not mean to refer so much to great exhibitions of skill and power as a diplomatist and a statesman, as to the qualities which belonged to him personally as a man, and which helped to grace and fill up the measure of his official character.

But this character for completeness to which I have alluded, may perhaps be better illustrated in the personal qualities which he exhibited in the amenities of private life. We have heard him called cold in his sympathies, and ungenial of manners, in his intercourse with others; and I confess that, till I knew him, I thought his seeming reserved, if not austere. But I need not say, in this presence, how soon this impression was corrected when one came in direct contact with him, either socially, or in the ordinary intercourse of private life. There was in his organization something of that shrinking delicacy which makes one apparently shy and sensitive. But I will venture to say, that no one ever went to him for kindness, or sympathy, or counsel, and found him either cold or repulsive.

He never forgot the courtesies of the gentleman in his intercourse with any man, however humble or devoid of influence he may have been. He never was surpassed in the scrupulous punctuality with which he replied to a correspondent, however unimportant the subject addressed to him, nor in the indulgence with which he received and the kindness with which he acknowledged, the well intended but often equivocal favor of printed works and papers, with which authors loaded his table and taxed his time — the thing he was the least able to spare.

The kindliness of his nature was manifested in a hundred different forms, though rarely so as to attract the observation or applause of others. In all the trying situations in which he was placed, at times, censured by party antagonism, misconstrued in his motives and his acts, and smarting under the keen rebuke of public disfavor, I do not believe any one ever saw him lose the dignity of his self possession, or heard him indulge in harsh or uncourteous language towards his bitterest opponent.

Nor will the world ever know how often the deserving young man, struggling with adverse circumstances, has found in him, what he needed more than money — a wise counsellor and a kind friend. Hundreds could now tell us how he sought them out, aided and encouraged them, and helped them onward in a career of usefulness and honor. While his body lay waiting for that august solemnity in which a whole city, and, I might add, a State and Nation bore a part, the door bell of his house was rung, and, upon its being opened, there stood upon the threshold a young man, a stranger, in the dress of a junior officer in the navy. He asked permission to come in and look, once more, upon the form and face of Mr.

Everett. " I am a stranger to you," said he to the gentleman in attendance, " but Mr. Everett was the best friend
I ever had; he procured me the place I now hold, and
from that day has never failed to write me letters of encouragement and advice, although I had no claim upon
his kindness and generosity."

Of his affluence, whether of wisdom or learning, of
worldly gifts or kindly consideration, he never withheld,
when appealed to by objects of merit and desert.

I desire also to say a single word upon another error
into which the public mind may have naturally fallen.
Whatever he wrote or delivered was, uniformly, so
finished and perfect in style and language, as well as in
thought, that an impression became general that he had
little ready or spontaneous eloquence, and that, in order
to meet an occasion, he must have time for careful preparation.   In the danger which he had to contend with, of
having himself for a rival, he was, undoubtedly, loth to
speak without previous preparation.   But his friends
knew that he was not only a man of ready and stirring
eloquence, but that, with all the grave, serious, and dignified manner which characterized so many of his orations
and public addresses, he had a fund of keen and sprightly
wit, of playful humor, and apt and gentle repartee, which,
at times, electrified the hour, and delighted whoever was
fortunate enough to witness them.

It might seem that for one who, through a long period
of public services, had shown himself worthy to hold a
place in the foremost rank, nothing could be needed to

fill up and round out a life of so much active usefulness and honor.

But do we not all feel, now, how much it would have wanted, if it had lacked the finish with which the history of the last four years has crowned and completed the work? Nobody had a right to doubt the honesty and sincerity of his convictions and opinions, however much one may have differed from him in the matters of public policy. But he saw the coming of that dreadful storm which has been sweeping over our country, and, like many other true patriots, he was willing to avert it by a conciliatory policy, though, by so doing, he subjected himself to the imputation of timidity or want of heart. But when he saw that the scheme of the conspirators was not to secure the rights which were theirs, but to usurp those to which they had no claim; when he saw that the purpose at which they aimed was not peace, but the overthrow, by war, of the Government under which our country had grown great and prosperous and happy, he threw the full weight of his accumulated power of intellect and influence into the struggle, and, in the forgetfulness of old opinions and cherished associations, he gave up to his country the stores of learning, the resources of eloquence, and the gathered energies of an entire life devoted to diligence and duty. Men no longer called him timid, for he showed that he had that highest of all courage, which dares to go against one's own prepossessions and uttered opinions, when in the light of present events, he looks back upon the unintentional mistakes of the past. The nation, the world itself looked on with admiration, as this brave old champion in the cause of right, urged on the battle by his trumpet call to duty and to arms.   And they felt that his record was complete, his life rounded out into the full proportions of Christian manliness, when he uttered that last noble appeal, to crown the triumphs of a nation's success, by the divine magnanimity that feeds our enemy and carries him comfort in the hour of prostration and distress.

While standing upon that lofty eminence of fame, to which a long and arduous life of noble action had raised him, it was a kind Providence that spared him from even the possibility of danger of any coming misapprehension or mistake.   He laid by his armor before the evening shadows had dimmed a single gleam of its brightness.   But he went not to his rest till his last day's work was fully and nobly accomplished.   He put off the garb which he had worn amid the dust and toil of an ever busy life, to waken to a new existence where, while the past is secure, the future can never be clouded by the passions of erring nature, or the frailties of human judgment.

The fame which, till then, had been in his own keeping, he left in charge of the country he had so long served.   And can we doubt that the trust will be sacredly kept?   They will rear to him statues and monuments. And they will do more.   They will keep these monuments and memorials alive, by cherishing the memory of the man to whom they are reared, in the treasured offerings of a nation's history.

It will be but another illustration of the immortality

27

which the fame of a truly great man lends to the works of art, by which men seek to perpetuate the memory of the dead. The chisel of the artist may bring out from the marble the form and features of one whom pride or affection may seek to honor. But it is, at last, to history that we must look, to interpret the record which sculpture may have tried to register.

You, sir, beautifully reminded us, on another occasion, of the search of the Roman orator amongst the rank weeds and gathered rubbish of the cemetery of Syracuse, for the forgotten monument of Archimedes, while you reminded his countrymen that the great American Philosopher and Statesman, till then, had no memorial of art reared to him, even in the city where he was born. But though they answered that appeal with a generous alacrity, the enduring bronze of which his speaking statue is fashioned by the skilful cunning of art, would do little to keep his memory alive for the service of posterity, if his name had not been enrolled among the great names that shed lustre upon the pages of his country's history.

So it will be with the statue which, as we trust, a gratified people will place by the side of his great compatriot, in the front of our Capitol. It is fitting that it should stand there, a memorial, immortal in the light of history, of the man, and of a people's gratitude. The name of Everett, repeated to the inquirer in after ages, will reanimate that form, and it will speak of the scholar, the statesman, the orator, the patriot, and the Christian gentleman, to whom it shall have been reared by a people that knew, and loved, and honored him.

The Rev. Mr. Waterston read the following communication from John G. Whittier, introducing the letter by the words of Dr. Channing, who said of Mr. Whittier, more than a quarter of a century ago: " His poetry bursts from the soul with the fire and energy of an ancient prophet. And his noble simplicity of character is the delight of all who know him."

AMESBURY, 27th 1st Month, 1865.

MY DEAR FRIEND: I acknowledge through thee, the invitation of the standing committee of the Massachusetts Historical Society to be present at a special meeting of the Society for the purpose of paying a tribute to the memory of our late illustrious associate, Edward Everett.

It is a matter of deep regret to me that the state of my health will not permit me to be with you on an occasion of so much interest.

It is most fitting that the members of the Historical Society of Massachusetts should add their tribute to those which have been already offered by all sects, parties, and associations, to the name and fame of their late associate. He was himself a maker of history, and part and parcel of all the noble charities and humanizing influences of his State and time.

When the grave closed over him who added new lustre to the old and honored name of Quincy, all eyes instinctively turned to Edward Everett as the last of that venerated class of patriotic civilians who, outliving all dissent and jealousy and party prejudice, held their reputation by the secure tenure of the universal appreciation of its worth as a common treasure of the republic. It is not for me to pronounce his eulogy. Others, better qualified by their intimate acquaintance with him, have done and will do justice to his learning, eloquence, varied culture, and social virtues. My secluded country life has afforded me few opportunities of personal intercourse with him, while my pronounced radicalism, on the great question which has divided popular feeling, rendered our political paths widely divergent. Both of us early saw the danger which threatened the country. In the language of the prophet, we " saw the sword coming. upon the land," but while he believed in the possibility of averting it by concession and compromise, I, on the contrary, as firmly believed that such a course could only strengthen and confirm what I regarded as a gigantic conspiracy against the rights and liberties, the union and the life, of the nation.

Recent events have certainly not tended to change this belief on my part ; but in looking over the past, while I see little or nothing to retract in the matter of opinion, I am saddened by the reflection, that through the very intensity of my convictions I may have done injustice to the motives of those with whom I differed. As respects Edward Everett, it seems to me that only within the last four years I have truly known him.

In that brief period, crowded as it is with a whole life-work of consecration to the union, freedom, and glory of his country, he not only commanded respect and reverence, but concentrated upon himself in a most remarkable degree the love of all loyal and generous hearts. We have seen, in these years of trial, very great sacrifices offered upon the altar of patriotism — wealth, ease, home-love, life itself. But Edward Everett did more than this; he laid on that altar not only his time, talents, and culture, but his pride of opinion, his long-cherished views of policy, his personal and political predilections and prejudices, his constitutional fastidious-ness of conservatism, and the carefully elaborated sym-metry of his public reputation. With a rare and noble magnanimity, he met, without hesitation, the demand of the great occasion. Breaking away from all the beset-ments of custom and association, he forgot the things that are behind, and, with an eye single to present duty, pressed forward towards the mark of the high calling of Divine Providence in the events of our time. All honor to him! If we mourn that he is now beyond the reach of our poor human praise, let us reverently trust that he has received that higher plaudit: "Well done, thou good and faithful servant!"

When I last met him, as my colleague in the Electoral College of Massachusetts, his look of health and vigor seemed to promise us many years of his wisdom and usefulness. On greeting him I felt impelled to express my admiration and grateful appreciation of his patriotic labors; and I shall never forget how readily and grace-fully he turned attention from himself to the great cause in which we had a common interest, and expressed his thankfulness that he had still a country to serve.

To keep green the memory of such a man is at once a

privilege and a duty.   That stainless life of seventy years is a priceless legacy. His hands were pure. The shadow of suspicion never fell on him. If he erred in his opinions (and that he did so, he had the Christian grace and courage to own), no selfish interest weighed in the scale of his judgment against truth.

As our thoughts follow him to his last resting-place, we are sadly reminded of his own touching lines, written many years ago at Florence. The name he has left behind is none the less " pure " that instead of being " humble," as he then anticipated, it is on the lips of grateful millions, and written ineffaceably on the record of his country's trial and triumph : —

> " Yet not for´ me when I shall fall asleep
> Shall Santa Croce's lamps their vigils keep;
> Beyond the main in Auburn's quiet shade,
> With those I loved and love my couch be made ; —
> Spring's pendent branches o'er the hillock wave,
> And morning's dewdrops glisten on my grave,
> While Heaven's great arch shall rise above my ·bed,
> When Santa Croce's crumbles on her dead —
> Unknown to erring or to suffering fame,
> So I may leave a pure though humble name "

Congratulating the Society on the prospect of the speedy consummation of the great objects of our associate's labors — the peace and permanent union of our country, —

I am very truly thy friend,

JOHN G. WHITTIER.

ROBERT C. WATERSTON, BOSTON.

The meeting then adjourned.

PROCEEDINGS

OF THE

THURSDAY-EVENING CLUB.

PROCEEDINGS OF THE THURSDAY-EVENING CLUB.

At a meeting of the Thursday-Evening Club, January 26, 1865, at the house of Mr. Gardner Brewer, the following remarks were made on the death of Mr. Everett, by Dr. J. Mason· Warren : —

Gentlemen: Since the last meeting of this Club, death has visited us; and, in the person of our friend and President, has called away the first citizen of our Commonwealth.

Honored alike at home and abroad, his loss will be felt throughout the length and breadth of the civilized world; and his name will justly stand among the most distinguished of all ages.

· Again and again, during the last week, has his eulogy been pronounced, in terms far more adequate to his merits than any which I can employ; yet here, in this circle of friends, we once more contemplate him in the private and social relation which he bore to this Association.

The peculiar organization of our Club — designed (to use the words of Mr. Everett, as spoken here on a former occasion) to bring together persons of different professions and pursuits, to converse and communicate with each other on the scientific improvements of the day, and other topics connected with social culture and progress; thus uniting the active and the professional, the scientific and business classes of the community in a friendly circle — has been successful, in no common degree, in combining refined social enjoyment with mutual improvement in knowledge.

The objects of such an Association were fully appreciated by Mr. Everett; and, from the very commencement of its meetings, his polished eloquence and rare conversational powers have greatly contributed to its success. Especially to be remembered are the noble eulogies in which he commemorated the removal by death of several prominent members of our Club; and we all remember, with gratitude and admiration, the splendid tribute, which, on the late decease of Mr. Frederic Tudor, he paid to the memory of the friend at whose house, only two weeks before, we had been so hospitably entertained. His illustrations of literary and historical subjects, with which he constantly favored us, are among the happiest reminiscences of our meetings; always felicitous in themselves, and often doubly impressive as emanating from one who had himself been an actor in the scenes which he described.

The first meeting of this season was held at his house, on the anniversary of the landing of our pilgrim forefathers ; and, in a style clear and masterly, even beyond his usual manner, he drew a new and vivid picture of that humble beginning of our national existence. Only a fortnight ago to-day, I received a note from him, regretting much that he was unable, owing to what he thought a slight illness, to be present at the meeting of that evening.

Of the punctuality with which, as President of the Club, he opened the meetings, you are all aware; for he well knew the value of time when measured by such results as he was accustomed to attain.

Feeling myself entirely incapable of doing justice to an occasion like this, I have yet been unwilling to let the evening pass without adding my feeble testimony to his entire faithfulness as a member and presiding officer of this Association. I leave to a gifted member of our Club the grateful task of giving fit expression to our sense of the great loss which we have sustained.

Mr. Edwin P. Whipple said : —

It is certainly fit, gentlemen, that the sense of bereavement which this city and the whole nation have felt in the death of Mr. Everett, should find emphatic expression in the Club of which he was the honored President. Known to every member as the most exquisitely affable of presiding officers ; a chairman with the gracious and graceful manners of a host; ever ready to listen as to speak ; and masking the eminence, which all were glad to acknowledge, in that bland and benignant courtesy, of which all were made to feel the charm, — his presence gave a peculiar dignity to our meetings which it will be impossible to replace, and impressed on all of us the conviction, that, to his other gifts and accomplishments, must be added the distinction of being the most accomplished gentleman of his time. Indeed, it is probable, that in this quality of high-bred and inbred courtesy, which we all have such good cause to admire and to remember, may be found the explanation and justification of some things in his character and career which have been subjected to adverse and acrimonious criticism ; and, in the few remarks I propose to make, allow me to throw into relations to this felicity of his nature, the powers and achievements which have made him so widely famous, and, what is better, so widely mourned.

Mr. Everett was born with that fineness of mental and of bodily organization, the sensitiveness of which is hardly yet thoroughly tolerated by the world which still profits by its superiorities. There was refinement in the very substance of his being ; by a necessity of his constitution he disposed everything he perceived into some orderly relations to ideas of dignity and grace ; he instinctively shunned what was coarse, discordant, uncomely, unbecoming ; and that internal world of thoughts, sentiments, and dispositions, which each man forms or re-forms for himself, and in which he really lives, in his case obeyed the law of comeliness, and came out as naturally in his manners as in his writings, in the beautiful urbanity of his behavior as in the cadenced periods of his eloquence. The fascination of this must have been felt even in his childhood, — for he was an orator whose infant prattle attracted an audience ; and he may be said to have passed from the cradle into public life. To a swiftness and accuracy of apprehension which made study the most delightful and self-rewarding of tasks, he added a general brightness, vigor, and poise of faculties, which gave premature promise of the reflection and judgment which were to come. By some sure instinct, the friends who seemed combined in a kindly conspiracy to assist and to spoil him, must have felt that they had to do with a nature whose innate modesty was its protection from conceit, and whose ambition to excel was but one form of its ambition for excellence. The fact to be considered is, that, in childhood and in youth as in manhood and age, there was something in him which irresistibly attracted admiration and esteem, and made men desirous of helping him on *in* the path his genius chose, and *to* the goal from which his destiny beckoned.

· It will be impossible here to do more than indicate the steps of that comprehensive career, so full of distinction for himself, so full of benefit to the nation, which has been for the past ten days the theme of so many eulogies: — the college student, bearing away the highest honors of his class; the boy-preacher, whose pulpit eloquence alternately kindled and melted men of maturest years ; the Greek Professor, whose knowledge of the finest and most flexible instrument of human thought extorted the admiration of the most accomplished of all the translators of Plato ; the fertile Writer and wide-ranging Critic, whose familiarity with many languages only added to the energy

and elegance with which he wielded the resources of his
own; the Representative of Middlesex, whose mastery of
the minutest details of political business was not more
evident than his ready grasp of the broader principles of
political science; the Governor of Massachusetts, whose
wise and able administration gave a new impulse to the
cause of education and to some of the most important of
the arts of peace; the Ambassador, who co-operated with
his friend, the great Secretary, in converting the provoca-
tions to what would have been one of the most calamitous
of all wars into the occasion for negotiating one of the
most beneficent of all treaties; the President of Harvard,
bringing back to his *Alma Mater* the culture he had
received from her increased an hundred fold, and present-
ing to the students the noble example of a scholarship
which was always teaching, and therefore always learning; the Secretary of State, whose brief possession of
office was yet sufficient to show with what firmness of
purpose he could uphold American honor, and with what
prodigality of information he could expound American
rights; the Orator of all " occasions," scattering through
many years, and from a hundred platforms, the rich stores
of his varied knowledge, the ripe results of his large
experience, and the animating inspirations of his fervid
soul; the Patriot, who ever made his scholarship, statesmanship, and eloquence serviceable and subsidiary to the
interest and glory of his country, and who, when would-
be parricides lifted their daggers to stab the august mother
who had borne them, flung himself, with a grand superiority to party prejudices, and a brave disdain of conse-

quences to himself, into the great current of impassioned purpose which surged up from the nation's heroic heart; the Christian philanthropist, who, through a long life, had been the object of no insult or wrong which could rouse in him the fierce desire for vengeance, and whose last public effort was a magnanimous plea for that "retaliation" which Christianity both allows and enjoins: — all these claims to honor, all this multiform and multiplied activity, have been the subjects of eager and emulous panegyric; and little has been overlooked in the loving and grateful survey.

Such a career implies the most assiduous self-culture; but it was a culture free from the fault of intellectual selfishness, for it was not centred in itself, but pursued with a view to the public service; and the thirst for acquisition was not stronger than the ardor for communication. Such a career also implies a constant state of preparation for public duties; but only by those whose ambition is to get office, rather than to get qualified for office, will this peculiarity be sneeringly imputed to a love of display. Still, the vast publicity which such a career rendered inevitable would have developed in him some of the malignant or some of the frivolous vices of public life, had it not been that a fine modesty tempered his constant sense of personal efficiency, — had it not been that a certain shyness at the core of his being made it impossible that his self-reliance should rush rudely out in any of the brazen forms of self-assertion. And this brings me back to that essential gentlemanliness of nature, which penetrated every faculty, and lent its tone to every expression of our departed President. This gave him a most sensitive regard for the rights and feelings of others, and this made him instinctively expect the same regard for his own. He guarded with an almost jealous vigilance the reserves of his individuality, and resented all uncouth or unwarranted intrusion into these sanctuaries which his dignity shielded, with a feeling of grieved surprise. In his wide converse with men, even in the contentions of party, his mind ever moved in a certain ideal region of mutual courtesy and respect. It was to be anticipated, that, in the rough game of politics, where blows are commonly given and received with equal carelessness, and where mutual charges of dishonesty are both expected and unheeded, such a nature as Mr. Everett's should sometimes suffer exquisite pain; that his nerves should quiver in impatient disgust of such odious publicity; that he should be tempted at times to feel that the inconsiderate assailers of his character —

> " Made it seem more sweet to be
> The little life of bank and brier,
> The bird that pipes his lone desire,
> And dies unheard within his tree—
>
> " Than he who warbles long and loud,
> And drops at Glory's temple-gates ;
> For whom the carrion-vulture waits
> To tear his heart before the crowd ! "

In this sensitiveness, refinement, and courtesy of nature, in this chivalrous respect for other minds, and tenderness for other hearts, is to be found the peculiarity of his oratory. He was the last great master of persuasive eloquence. The circumstances of the time have given to our public speaking an aggressive and denouncing character, and invective has contemptuously cast persuasion aside, and almost reduced it to the condition of one of the lost arts. This is undoubtedly a great evil, for invective commonly dispenses with insight, is impotent to interpret what it assails, and fits the tongue of mediocrity as readily as that of genius. It is true that the mightiest exemplars of eloquence have been those who have wielded this most terrific weapon in the armory of the orator with the most overwhelming effect. Demosthenes, Chatham, Burke, Mirabeau, men of vivid minds, hot hearts, and audacious wills, have made themselves the terror of the assemblies they ruled, by their power of uttering those brief and dreadful invectives, which " appall the guilty and make bold the free," — which come like the lightning, irradiating *for* an instant what *in* an instant they blast. Perhaps the noblest spectacle in the annals of eloquence is that in which the mute rage and despair of a hundred millions of Asiatics found, in the assembly responsible for their oppression, fiery utterance from the intrepid lips of Burke. But such men are rightly examples only to their peers; a certain autocracy of nature is the animating principle of their genius; and, when they are copied simply by the tongue, they are likely to produce shrews rather than sages. Mr. Everett followed the bent of his character and the law of his mind when he aimed to enter into genial relations with his auditors, and to associate the reception

29

of his views with a quickening of their better feelings, and an addition to their self-respect. Mount Vernon, the poor of East Tennessee, the poor of Savannah, attest that his greatest triumphs were those of persuasion. And in recalling the tones of that melodious voice, whose words were thus works, one is tempted to think that Force, in eloquence, is the mailed giant of the feudal age, who, assailing under a storm of missiles the fortress of his adversary, makes the tough gates shiver under the furiously rapid strokes of his battle-axe, and enters as a victor; while Persuasion, " with his garland and singing robes about him," speaks the magical word which makes the gates fly open of their own accord, and enters as a guest.

It is but just, gentlemen, that our lamented President, the source of so many eulogies, should now be their theme; that his joy in recognizing eminency in others should be met by a glad and universal recognition of it in himself. And, certainly, that spotless private and distinguished public life could have closed at no period when the heart of the whole loyal nation was more eager to admire the genius of the orator, and sound the praises of the patriot, and laud the virtues of the man, than on the day when his mortal frame, beautiful in life and beautiful in death, was followed by that long procession of bereaved citizens, through those mourning streets, to that consecrated grave!

Bishop Eastburn said : —

I ask the indulgence of my fellow-members of the Club for a few moments, while I add to the eloquent words that have been spoken, my own humble tribute to the memory of our late illustrious President. Mr. Everett was kind enough once to say to me, that he wished I would sometimes offer something, at these meetings, as a contribution towards the instruction of those who should be present. My reply to him was, that, surrounded as I always found myself here by so much science and wisdom, I felt disposed rather to sit as a silent listener; and I cannot help a solemn and tender feeling in the reflection, that when now, for the first time, I am complying with his request, it is to utter a few words of remembrance over his recently opened grave.

I beg to call your attention, gentlemen, in the few words I shall say, to one or two points in Mr. Everett's illustrious career which have not been dwelt upon by the speakers who have just addressed us, — and which seem to me to present him in an aspect eminently worthy of study by the rising youth of this nation.

I very often thought, during the life of our distinguished President, and have thought more especially since his death, of the shining example he has set of the assiduous cultivation of classical learning, as the chief ingredient in efficient education, and as the great means of giving superior abilities a commanding influence over men. It was this that gave the charm to Mr. Everett's oratory, and carried home with power his advocacy, as a statesman, of public measures, and his addresses in behalf of those efforts for the relief of suffering humanity to which he devoted the closing years of his life. He seemed to enter fully into those views of the advantage of classical pursuits put forth by the great Sir Robert Peel, in a discourse delivered by him on being installed as Lord Rector of the University of Glasgow, and which I remember reading many years ago, — where he speaks of the benefits of classical, as distinguished from mere mathematical training; and shows the tendency of the latter to narrow the mind, and to indispose it, in regard to a certain class of subjects, to receive any other than a species of evidence of which these subjects are not susceptible. But, besides this, Sir Robert exhibited, in a striking manner, the inestimable value of the study of the great masters, by a review of the course of Cicero, whose wonderful oratory received its perfection, and its power of swaying men, from his cultivation of the great models of Grecian poetry and eloquence. Now Mr. Everett, as I have said, is a great example in this respect, and ought to be held up as such before the young men of this land. And, if he shall be generally followed, we shall hear less, in the pulpit, on the platform, and on deliberative floors, of that rant and bombast which pass with some for eloquence, but which are as offensive to good taste as they are barren of effect. Mr. Bullock, in his address at Faneuil Hall on the day before the funeral of our departed President, dwelt with great force and eloquence upon this way in which Mr. Everett trained himself for influence, — showing that his classical finish was not something standing by itself, and apart from his distinction as a statesman, but was the main element in creating that distinction, and in giving him the power which he possessed in his signal public career. And, gentlemen, who has not felt the control exerted by his brilliant, yet restrained, chastened, and simple diction? His oratory, sparkling with ornament as it was, was at the same time a perfect specimen of the *simplex munditiis*. So that, whenever we heard him, it was like looking at some noble Grecian temple, in the presence of which the eye is not distracted hither and thither by tawdry and vulgar details, but takes in at once the exquisite *whole*, and is charmed with the beauty of its architectural lines, and the fair symmetry of its proportions.

But, before I sit down, allow me to detain you for a few moments longer by reminding you of another feature of Mr. Everett's career, which ought to be impressed on the youth of this country. I refer to the fact, that this great man achieved his triumphs, and produced the results which we have witnessed, by a life of constant and laborious industry. He eminently taught by his example, that they who would either attain eminence, or, what is infinitely more important, would urge mankind onward to noble purposes, must not rely upon the native genius with which God has gifted them, but must discipline their faculties by unremitted labor. My first sight of Mr. Everett was forty-three years ago, when, in 1822, he came to New York to deliver the Sermon at the opening of a place of worship of his denomination. I had not then entered on my own professional course; and, with the curiosity and enthusiasm of a youth desirous of getting a near sight of so eminent a man, — for even then he was eminent, although but twenty-eight years of age, — I took a position, after the service was over, in the porch, in order that I might study his countenance as he passed out into the street; — and, as he walked by me with his slender form, in gown and band, with his curling auburn hair, and his fine contour of head and features, I thought him the most attractive specimen of radiant classical beauty I had ever beheld in my life. Now, gentlemen, many of us have been witnesses of his course from that morning of his life down to its recent close. And what has this course been? Has it been an indolent resting upon the consciousness of great natural endowments? No. Has it been a course marked by fitful and impulsive resort to study? No. It has been a life of unintermitted labor — of continual storing of the mind — of daily addition to that wealth of resources which was to be the instrument of power. I have touched upon this feature of Mr. Everett's distinguished life, because, as I have already observed, I think it should be placed distinctly before the young men of this country; showing them for their instruction, that influence, and consequent usefulness, come not from intellect alone, however marvellous, but from intellect disciplined, regulated, and made efficient, by the toil which 'scorns delights, and lives laborious days.'

I thank you for the permission to present these thoughts to your attention; for I felt that I could not refrain from adding my humble tribute to this remarkable man, here in one of those assemblies which he has so often adorned with his presence, and charmed with the contributions of his eloquent lips.

Dr. A. A. Gould said : —

I am sure that each one of us here associated must feel thankful to the gentlemen who have so faithfully and gratefully delineated the exalted character of our late President, and especially as they recall to us his interest in our meetings, and the many contributions he himself made for our entertainment and edification. The breaking out of the rebellion bore so heavily on his health and spirits, that he expressed some misgivings as to his ability to meet with us, and even as to the judiciousness of continuing the meetings of the Club. At the preliminary meeting this year, however, he seemed quite enthusiastic in view of our coming entertainments ; and you will all of you attest to the peculiar geniality with which he opened our winter's gatherings at his own house.

I venture to propose, what I have no doubt will find an affirmative response from every one, that the gentlemen who have addressed us be requested to furnish copies of their remarks, to be transmitted to the family of our late President, as a testimonial, from the members of this Club, of their deep sense of indebtedness to him for his countenance, and his numerous instructive and entertaining contributions at their meetings, as well as of his exalted private worth and public eminence.

PROCEEDINGS

OF THE

NEW ENGLAND HISTORIC-GENEALOGICAL SOCIETY.

30

NEW ENGLAND HISTORIC-GENEALOGICAL SOCIETY.

A special meeting of the Board of Directors of the New England Historic-Genealogical Society was held on Tuesday afternoon, January 17, 1865, to take notice of the death of the Hon. Edward Everett, a member of the Society from the year of its organization. William B. Towne was called to the chair, and William Reed Deane was appointed secretary *pro tempore.*

John H. Sheppard, the librarian, introduced the subject by these remarks : —

THE sudden death of the Hon. Edward Everett has called us together not merely to testify our deep sorrow for the loss of a most influential and honored member of our Society, but, with other numerous institutions, to offer our humble tribute of respect to the memory of a very eminent man of our common country. A great light has gone down in our political heavens; a star of the first magnitude, admired at home and among foreign nations, whose brilliant rays of science and eloquence have adorned this Western Hemisphere and made a luminous path, has set forever. Our nation has met with an irreparable loss, and particularly in these dark days and troublous times of an unholy rebellion, when his counsels and voice are so much needed. His death has cast a gloom over society through the length and breadth of the land. It will be felt in the Cabinet, in the national and legislative halls, on the battle-field, and everywhere; for his eloquence was everywhere heard, as it were, on the wings of the press, speaking with the voice of one going about to do good; and in no place will his death be more lamented than in a sister city, to relieve which the very last hours of his exceedingly busy and energetic life were devoted; yes, the tears of Savannah will gush forth at the sad news.

Mr. Everett has left us a striking example that old age does not necessarily impair the intellectual powers, when they have been vigorously kept in exercise. In his seventy-first year, his talents were bright and active as ever, and his judgment and imagination retained the full power of his earlier days. He was, indeed, *in se ipso totus, teres atque rotundus;* there was a wholeness, a polish, and a round-ness in his character, wherein all the rough edges and sharp angles so often met with, even among distinguished men, were softened into a pleasing smoothness. On this melancholy occasion we can only present a few resolu-tions, echoing the words of universal sorrow; and though they cannot add to the fame of the illustrious dead, yet they may evince our grief and sympathy.

Mr. Sheppard then offered the following resolutions : —

Resolved, That, in the death of Hon. Edward Everett, this Society, of which he was a resident member for nineteen years, deplores a great loss.

Resolved, That, in his death, literature and science are called to mourn the departure of a very distinguished scholar and accomplished writer, whose purity and elegance of taste, richness of imagination, affluence of language, and flowing, fascinating style, would, without any other mark of distinction or celebrity, have made him an honor and an ornament to our country.

Resolved, That, in his death, the voice of a most eloquent man is silent, — a voice which left no superior, if, indeed, it did an equal in this land, and which was ever exerted in the cause of all that is good or excellent, pertaining to a nation's welfare.

Resolved, That, in the death of this statesman and patriot, the whole nation has reason to weep and lament; for his exalted love of the Union gave to his voice and counsels a peculiar importance in the present great struggle to preserve our nationality from destruction.

Resolved, That, in his death, we deplore the loss of a citizen of most exemplary virtues, indefatigable industry, and faithful adherence to those noble principles of justice and honor, from the prevalence only of which a nation can become great and glorious.

Resolved, That we respectfully tender our sympathies to the bereaved family.

Resolved, That, in testimony of our veneration of the memory of the deceased, we will attend his funeral on Thursday next; and also, that a copy of these Resolutions be presented to his family.

After remarks by Samuel G. Drake, Rev. Elias Nason, John H. Sheppard, Frederic Kidder, John Ward Dean, William B. Trask, William Reed Deane, and the presiding officer, the Resolutions were unanimously adopted.

PROCEEDINGS

OF THE

AMERICAN ANTIQUARIAN SOCIETY.

PROCEEDINGS OF THE AMERICAN ANTIQUA-RIAN SOCIETY,

The members having been notified of the death of their former President, Hon. Edward Everett, assembled in their Hall at two o'clock, P. M. Hon. Stephen Salisbury, the President, occupied the chair. On account of the illness of Hon. Levi Lincoln, whose relations with Mr. Everett had been many and important, the meeting was adjourned to Governor Lincoln's residence. After calling the Society to order the President spoke as follows : —

BRETHREN OF THE AMERICAN ANTIQUARIAN SOCIETY : —

While the voices of our people express their sorrow and deep concern that one of our most exalted citizens, who swayed the opinions and destiny of our country from a sphere above the distractions of political life and the envious assaults with which public office is infested, I have invited you to assemble here, not to forget your duties and interests as citizens, but to remember that this little company of students of history and antiquarian lore have lost their honored Ex-President, Edward Everett, the associate who had the greatest present ability to promote the objects of your association. The eloquence

31

that honored the obsequies of the Nestor of your Society, the Hon. Josiah Quincy, still reëchoes in your printed proceedings, meeting a cordial reception wherever learning, virtue, and a laborious, conscientious, and beneficent life are held in honor. He stood among us in the majesty and gathered wisdom of 94 years, and his wise counsels faltered on his lips when he heard the summons for which he waited and hastened away. And now a second time the solemn warning of Providence has addressed this Society, and from the clear sky in which no threatening cloud was apparent, another distinguished leader of this fraternity has been struck down. The last act of his life was to plant sweet Christian charity among the sufferings and crimes of wicked and treacherous rebellion, and this effort is a possible cause of his sudden, and, as we in our ignorance and impatience are prone to say, his untimely departure. Let us rather repeat the familiar words of the old Roman, that " he was not more happy in the glory of his life than in the occasion of his death." But I will not detain you with my own unsatisfactory words from the utterance of thoughts more worthy of your own feelings and of the occasion. In my desire to forward the deliberations of the hour, I will venture to offer the following resolutions : —

The American Antiquarian Society, being convened to take notice of the sudden death of their honored Ex-President, Edward Everett, LL. D., who was for nine years Secretary for foreign Correspondence, and afterwards for twelve years the President, it was thereupon

Resolved, That we deeply sympathize in the universal

grief of our country, that a patriot has been taken away in the fullest strength and glory of his beneficent service, and his mantle is not seen to fall on any successor.

Resolved, That with our lamentations for a great public loss, we will gratefully consider the noble works which he has recently performed in the defence of our government and our national privileges; in the vindication of the right and the safety of free institutions, and in the thrice repeated lessons of charity and Christian forgiveness, enforced by his own unequalled and persuasive example.

Resolved, That we will embalm with the odor of our exalted praise the memory of an orator who always carried his admiring listeners to higher and happier planes of thought; a scholar of incessant and unwearied labor, who brought up his deep-sought treasures with a fitness and polish that adapted them to the handling and uses of common life, and a man who exercised his great powers for useful ends with a kind and cautious prudence and constant regard for Christian purity.

Resolved, That it is our privilege to offer a chaplet of honor and fraternal grief at the tomb of our Ex-President, who gave to this Society the advantage of the highest official relations for twenty-one years, and has since been a fellow-worker by his constant contributions, and especially by his frequent and successful pursuit of the objects for which this association was formed.

Resolved, That we offer to the children of our respected associate our sincere condolence, and commend them to the highest Source of consolation.

Resolved, That as a Society, we will express our respect by attending the funeral of Mr. Everett on Thursday the 19th instant.

Resolved, That the President of this Society is requested to transmit a copy of the above resolutions to the family of our deceased associate.

The resolutions having been seconded by Rev. Seth Sweetser, D.D., the chair was addressed by Dr. Sweetser, Rev. Dr. Alonzo Hill, Hon. Isaac Davis, Hon. Ira M. Barton, Hon. Levi Lincoln, and Hon. Henry Chapin; after which the resolutions were unanimously adopted.

Rev. Dr. Sweetser spoke in substance as follows : —

Mr. President: It seems hardly fitting that I should occupy a moment of the time of this meeting. My relations with the distinguished ex-president of this Society were not such as to justify it. It has not been my privilege to come within the circle of his friendship, or to be associated with him, as others here present have been, in public services. It would be presumptuous in me to speak of a personal acquaintance with Mr. Everett. And yet, sir, in common with the multitude of his friends, I have felt an admiration for his character and attainments.

Since the intelligence of his sudden death reached and saddened us, my thoughts have been carried back to the period of my first knowledge of him. At the time of my entering college he occupied the chair of Greek Literature in Harvard University, and I well remember the enthusiasm which he kindled, and the admiration with

which he inspired those who listened to him, and how his
lecture-room was thronged; and I remember also what
deep regret was felt by the whole college at his with-
drawal from the Professorship, which took place soon
after.

We were young and not fitted to appreciate the capacity
of such a mind, or to measure the fulness and richness
of his classical culture, or the beauty and art with which
he displayed the intellectual and literary treasures of
that land of beauty and art which, to this day, has never
found a rival.

It was the universal feeling that the department and
the college itself had lost the service of one who, by his
varied attainments and scholarship, was eminently fitted
to elevate the tone of classical learning, and inspire an
interest in the literature of Greece. The regret was
general, and I cannot refrain from saying, that with me
it has never ceased. But, sir, though removed to the stir
and agitating scenes of public life, his eminent abilities
were not lost. I will not speak of his services in the
important positions which he has occupied in the State
and the Nation. There are other gentlemen here who
are better able to do that than I am. I will speak only
of his scholarship.

He was always a scholar. He was a student in the
fullest sense of the word. He never failed in his allegiance to scholarship. Under all circumstances he exhibited the same purity and richness, the same grace and
elegance. Everything he did was done in the spirit and
tone of a true scholarship. Whether he addressed the

senate or the popular assembly, or spoke in associations of literary and scientific men, or in the courts of law, there was the same completeness and accuracy. Whatever was possible to diligence and assiduous culture he attained. Whatever could be accumulated by persistent research he acquired.

. . . .

We have not been in the habit of looking upon Mr. Everett as possessing that boldness and force which push out beyond the ordinary range of thought; we have not classed him with the minds which extend the boundaries of human knowledge. He was not of that adventurous wing which shoots up above the flight and sight of other men. But if he had not these qualities he had what is perhaps more worthy of honor and admiration. He had the power of acquiring and accumulating, the faculty of retaining, arranging, and using, whatever could be gathered up by unwearied and diversified study. He was everything that labor and severe training, and the unfaltering pursuit of his object could make him.

. . . .

Some years since Mr. Everett was invited, as gentlemen in his position frequently are, to address the Massachusetts Bible Society at an anniversary meeting in Boston. I heard him on that occasion. He spoke from the platform as other gentlemen did, connecting his remarks with those of previous speakers, giving the usual appearance of extemporaneousness to his address.

A friend asked him for his notes, and his manuscript was, I apprehend, an index to all his performances. It was carefully written and elaborated; words were selected with great skill and discrimination; some were erased and others inserted in their stead; and this exactness in the choice of language, in some instances, was carried to the fourth and fifth erasure. This was one of the sources of his success. He never trusted to the uncertainty of hasty unpremeditated utterances. He finished and perfected with accuracy and the most studious art. He spared no toil or pains in preparation. He always knew his subject, his audience, and the occasion. It was in this way that he was so successful as a public speaker. The rich stores of his classical reading and the treasures of literature and science were at his disposal. His wide cultivation, and the perfection of his exercise in speech, enabled him to express in the most persuasive and eloquent form the instructions he imparted.

Now that he is no more with us, as we recall his genius, his acquisitions, his diligence, we look back upon him as furnishing to us and coming generations an unsurpassed model in the art of eloquence.

This Society, as an association of scholars, the university which nurtured him, all lovers of good learning, the whole republic of letters, the Commonwealth which gave him birth, and which he so nobly served, and the whole country, owe to him a debt of honor and of gratitude.

He has been suddenly taken from us. It is not for us to question the propriety of the time of his departure; but for this we have occasion to be thankful, that he was not taken until he had rendered a service to his country in its great perils which endears him to the heart of every

true lover of the Union, and which will prove the freshest
and most enduring brightness in the chaplet of his future
renown.

Rev. Dr. Hill said : —

MR. PRESIDENT : Since the death of Mr. Adams in the
rotunda of our Capitol, in Washington, seventeen years
ago, no event has produced so profound a sensation as
the sudden demise of the revered ex-president of this
Society. When Mr. Webster died he had lingered ; and
his death was not unexpected nor unprepared for. But
Mr. Everett passed in a moment from the midst of the
activities of life, while his mind was teeming with mighty
projects of usefulness, while his last noble speech in
behalf of forgiveness and charity and the pacification of
the country, was still throbbing on the telegraph wires
and thrilling the heart of a continent.

I did not know him intimately, — perhaps few did.
But my memory goes far back in his personal history ; I
have followed him with admiration and been held captive
by the power of his soft persuasion, with thousands of
others, to the last. I have heard him in the pulpit ; and
his youthful figure, cut with classical elegance and set
forth with the high polish of art, as he stood in the desk
of the college chapel, is still before me ; and whole passages of his sermons on those occasions, fascinating with
their splendid rhetoric and pronounced with inimitable
grace of utterance, are still fresh in my recollection. I
was among the privileged few who heard his brilliant
course of lectures on Greek Literature on his return from

Athens, whose delivery marked for us a new era in our mental history. I have listened to most, and have read all of his more elaborate orations, delivered at different periods, on almost every variety of subjects, and have always come away from the hearing or the reading his debtor. I have been present for several years at the meetings of literary and benevolent associations of which he was a member, and have noticed his fidelity, the readiness with which he consecrated his great powers to their welfare, and the intelligence and earnest devotion with which he attended to the little details connected with their prosperity. I wish to say a few words here as a grateful tribute to his memory.

Many years ago, when he was a very young man, he was addressing an assembly of Boston merchants whom he had invited to meet him at Faneuil Hall, and whom he was endeavoring to persuade to purchase for the use of Harvard College, a work of art, the Panorama of Athens, I think it was, which had just arrived from Greece. He was showing the value of art in a young community like our own, and in the course of his argument put the question into the mouth of his hearers, " What is it good for ? " I shall never forget the force of manner and expression which he threw into his reply, put also into the form of a question, " What is anything good for except as it refines and ennobles and brings out the divine in man ? " Here we have the key-note which guided, the undertone which sounded through his whole subsequent life. In all his speeches, written and unwritten, in all the works that he did through a period of fifty years, how have they

32

conspired for the uplifting and refining of our nature. Point to the word, if you can, employed to disguise the truth, or suggest the thought which one might not breathe into the ears of saintly purity.   Put your finger, you cannot, upon the passage set round with the spears and darts of detraction, serving to arouse a base passion and to make us less humane.   How many will you find, all scattered through his living example and published works, which are a noble appeal to our higher sentiments, and make us love with a deeper sensibility whatever is beautiful in nature and refined in life.   Early moulded by the models of Grecian art and culture, familiar with the best thoughts and noblest sentiments of all ages, sparing no labor to perfect what he undertook to say and do, he poured forth his honeyed accents, lifted up, electrified, and melted us by the gorgeous imagery and beautiful drapery with which he clothed his thought — but touched us the more deeply because of this undertone of high Christian sentiment which breathed, and this coloring of Christian faith and hope which glowed, through his best productions.

How broad, how varied, were his accomplishments. He seems to have studied every subject, and gone to its depths.   Read his lectures before the Mechanics', the Mercantile, and Library Associations, his addresses before Agricultural Societies, and his debates in Congress.   He goes into the details of science, the theory of trade, the methods of raising crops, and the ways of public policy, as if each profession had been his especial pursuit and he had devoted himself to nothing else.   He shows a surprising familiarity with every department of knowledge, and speaks of its practical working as if he had been engaged in the occupation all his life. But he does more than this. He goes into the soul of the thing, and shows how the mechanic and the merchant, the farmer and legislator, may transform their callings into liberal pursuits and make them tributary to the individual growth and the moral and spiritual elevation of the community.

So also in the refined integrity of his life, his sympathy with the fine arts, and the devotion of his rich accomplishments to the ornament of the Republic, we see the same great aim throughout. He was the friend of Canova, and the intimate of some of the most gifted of the modern poets. He was practised in modern languages so that he could talk with the ambassadors at the court of St. James, each in his own tongue. He had carefully studied in the galleries of art, and in the associations in London commanded, it is said, high respect for the accuracy of his judgment and taste, and was an authority there among the lovers of painting and sculpture. But here he was true too to the early expressed purpose of his life. He was no hermit. He did not keep his high gifts for his own uses and enjoyment; but spread them abroad, as a sweet fragrance, for all who would receive them. No man was summoned so often as he, to speak to his fellow-citizens — to interpret the meaning of great historical events and mould them to the time; and no man could do more to make them memorable by the vividness of his imagination and the affluence of his speech. Though he spoke so often, to hear Mr. Everett was an era in one's life.

Pictures were drawn upon the tablets of the heart, never to be erased; for with him eloquence was a divine endowment, and must be used only to refine, elevate, and perfect the soul of man.

For, as I have already intimated, I do not believe he ever forgot his accountability for his great gifts, or relaxed in his reverence for all that is Christian in belief and spiritual in life and hope. He seemed to me to lean more than most great men for personal guidance and support on the influence of his traditionary faith. Early attracted by the fascination and fervid friendship of young Buckminster, whose successor he was, at the unripe age of nineteen, over the most influential congregation in Boston, he never forgot his first love, nor wavered in his attachment to Christian institutions and the means of Christian culture; but through a varied experience at home and abroad, under circumstances of great temptation, remained true to his early convictions — showing by the consistency and integrity of his daily walk the depth of those convictions. When I have preached in the church in which he worshipped, he was always there, forenoon and afternoon — devout, reverential, and bending his active and affluent mind to a part in the services. He did not, I thought, occupy his pew merely for example's sake; but sat lowly, as needing help like the rest of us — composed in prayer, and when the lesson of the day was read — true also to his scholarly habits, following it in the Greek Testament, which he kept by his side. This may seem a small matter, but it means much. For when I remember how often great scholars, surrounded by their rich libraries, attract-

ed by the fascination of letters, and borne on the tide of
popularity and abundant success, sufficient of themselves,
have been allured away from the highest objects of interest, I can honor the illustrious man, who remained steadfast to the offices of the Church, and confessed his
need of ministrations which have been the guide and
solace of those who possessed no book but one ; — ministrations which have done so much for the good order,
moral and spiritual strength of New England, and made
her what she is.   Mr. Everett was never seduced by his
classical studies nor the philosophies of the day from the
deeper philosophy of Jesus of Nazareth, but by the
greatness of the contrast could all the more appreciate
the unrivalled beauty and grandeur of his simplest utterances; and so when the cry of woe came up from the
bosom of those who had just now been our enemies, and
a plea must be made for forgiveness and charity, he found
no fitting language in heathen poet or orator — but
repeated with a pathos and power which moved the vast
assembly who heard, the words in which the great apostle
has embodied the very soul of his Master, " If thine
enemy hunger feed him.   If he thirst give him drink."
For the last time he spoke in the name and spirit of
Christ, and never had he spoken so persuasively.

But he has gone.   In the silence of the night, before
the Sabbath dawned, the great soul, that never tired
before, went to its rest.   And you have done well, Mr.
President, in your admirable remarks, to quote in their
English dress the fitting words of Tacitus, with whom he
was so familiar — " *Felix non vitæ tantum claritate sed*

etiam opportunitate mortis.". He is gone, the finished scholar, the consummate orator, the consistent Christian; and he should sleep to-day, as Prescott, dying, expressed a wish to do in his, in that magnificent library — which has been the scene of his vigils, his labors, and his successes. To-day, lying in his sacred repose, he should be surrounded by the noble array of scholars, artists, and poets, who, having inspired him in life, might look down upon him from the alcoves and walls of that library, in the stillness of death.   To-morrow, friends will tenderly bear him to Mount Auburn, where his masters and early companions have gone before, and where living scholars and a grateful people will go to mourn over and catch inspiration from the foremost man that has been among us.

Hon. Isaac Davis spoke thus : —

Mr. President : The sad and solemn dispensation of Divine Providence, which has so suddenly removed from earth to his eternal home one of the brightest ornaments of our race, touches the sensibilities and awakens the sympathies of scholars and statesmen, poets and orators, patriots and freemen, — of all who read or speak the English tongue.

Scarcely has the tomb closed over the remains of one of the most gifted sons of Massachusetts, who was a member of this Society, when it again opens to receive a ripe scholar, a distinguished orator, a devoted patriot and Christian gentleman, who was for many years its President.

Few men of our country — very few — will fill so large a space in the history of the nineteenth century as Edward Everett. At the early age of seventeen he was graduated at Harvard University with its highest honors ; and first turning his attention to theology, became pastor of one of the largest churches in Boston. The Professorship of Greek Literature having been tendered to him by his Alma Mater, with the privilege of visiting Europe to qualify himself more fully for the office, he resigned his pastorate at the age of twenty and repaired to the University of Göttingen, where for two years he assiduously pursued the studies connected with the duties of the new office. He afterwards visited Greece and other parts of Europe ; and returning to America at the age of twenty-five entered upon the labors of his professorship. He soon became editor of the North American Review, which under his care attained to its highest reputation and widest circulation ; while his lectures on Greek literature and art gave him great distinction as a profound and finished scholar. In 1824, before the Phi Beta Kappa Society of the University, he commenced that series of public addresses on various subjects which have given him such an exalted fame as an orator. He was elected to Congress by the unsolicited votes of the citizens of Middlesex in the same year ; and for ten years was a working member, prominent among the distinguished men, of that body. He retired from Congress, and for four successive years was elected Governor of Massachusetts. In 1841, he was appointed Minister to the Court of St. James, where he remained four years.

While in England his accomplishments became known to statesmen and scholars. They were recognized by the Universities of Cambridge and Oxford; each conferring upon him the honorary degree of D. C. L., a distinction which, I believe, had been conferred by them on no other American citizen. In 1846, he was chosen President of Harvard University, and devoted himself to the discharge of the delicate and responsible duties of that office till his resignation in 1849. On the death of Mr. Webster he was appointed Secretary of State of the United States. On a change of Administration he took his seat in the Senate of the United States as successor to Hon. John Davis, who had succeeded him as President of this Society. In 1854, he was compelled by the state of his health to retire to private life. In his orations on the life and character of Washington subsequently delivered, he faithfully and eloquently warned the citizens of the Republic against secession or disunion and all their attendant consequences.

These are some of the incidents in the life of this great man. Edward Everett is dead; but the influence of his genius and industry will live in all coming generations till the last succession of earth's inhabitants.

Judge Barton said : —

I desire Mr. President, merely to allude to my early recollections of Mr. Everett, as illustrating the justness of the remarks of the Rev. Drs. Sweetser and Hill, as to his prominent characteristics as a scholar and a man. Those recollections are amongst my most cherished memories, running back to the year 1820, when I entered the Law School of Harvard University.

Mr. Everett had then just returned from his foreign travels, and a residence at one of the German Universities, preparatory to entering upon his duties as Professor of Greek literature. He had previously ministered with great distinction in the Brattle Street Church, Boston; and I first saw him as the officiating clergyman in the College Chapel at Cambridge. It was said to be his first appearance there after his return home. And now, after a lapse of more than forty years, it may be of some interest to note, that the text from which he discoursed was the familiar and beautiful scripture, " The lines have fallen unto *us* in pleasant places," &c. The discourse demonstrated, that while his taste had received the highest culture, his love for his country had not, as is sometimes the case, been impaired by absence from it.

The lectures of Mr. Everett on Greek literature, and of Professor Ticknor on Spanish and French literature, were in progress; and by a wise regulation of the College, the members of the Law School, as resident graduates, were allowed to attend them. They were of the purest models of English composition ; and those who failed to improve from such exemplars, must have been wanting either in taste or attention.

Mr. Everett, though then a young man, but two or three years my senior, had already acquired a literary distinction sufficient to satisfy the ordinary aspiration of scholars, as a reward for the literary labors of a whole

33

life. Nevertheless, he continued to be a most diligent student. By a pleasant and noteworthy coincidence, he had for his study one of the spacious drawing rooms of the Craigie House, occupied by General Washington, while in Cambridge, as his Head-Quarters. Decorated with a large painting of the Colosseum at Rome, and other illustrations of ancient works of art. When he came from his study, Mr. Everett was always prepared for the occasion on which he was to appear, whether before the students or the public. He never trusted to the inspiration of the moment for his thoughts or words. And yet his performances never appeared finical nor constrained. He had thus early acquired that most desirable literary accomplishment, " the art of concealing art." We all know the great care and labor he bestowed on his public literary performances in after life, as graphically described by Dr. Sweetser. Yet his auditors would never suspect the fact ; but would take all he eloquently said as the instant promptings of his subject and the occasion.

The studious and somewhat retired habits of Mr. Everett, and perhaps his superior position amongst his fellows, sometimes led to the remark that he was unsocial in his feelings. If by that was meant that he was courteous and dignified in his manners, and that he had little time or taste for mere commonplace conversation, such remark had the semblance of truth. But if anything more was meant, the assertion was the reverse of the truth.

At the period referred to, there was a club of junior officers of the College and resident graduates, for improvement in elocution, and to socialize the young men, many of whom came together as strangers from different parts of the country. Mr. Everett was the originator and inspiring genius of the Association. On one occasion he recited, with amusing effect, the humorous dialogue found in the schoolbooks of the day, between three travellers, on the color of the chameleon : —

> " Oft has it been my lot to mark
> A proud, conceited, talking spark,
> Returning from his finished tour," &c.

The circumstance of his own recent return from a four or five years' tour, with his effective recital of the dialogue, put the Association on very good terms with the speaker, and with each other. And I am not aware that any one afterwards imputed to our distinguished associate any improper reserve or austerity of manners.

With extraordinary natural talents, and such habits of study, added to a fine person and melodious voice, the friends of Mr. Everett might safely predict for him a successful and brilliant literary career. They were not disappointed. He soon became the learned man of the country. To say nothing of his public services, properly so called, by his connection and coöperation with numerous religious, charitable, and literary institutions, at home and abroad, he conferred upon his country an honor, equalled only by the distinction he secured to himself.

It was a wise choice when Mr. Everett was elected the presiding officer of this Society. For though not devoted to American antiquities as a specialty, he was distinguished for his antiquarian knowledge, as it related to both the old and the new world. And he brought to our aid, not merely his great reputation as a general scholar, but much learning appropriate to our peculiar department of literature.

Mr. President, one reason for the success of Mr. Everett in performing the duties of life, should not be forgotten. It was his early education in Christian theology. Small and unprincipled men, for their own selfish purposes, sometimes attempted his disparagement, by reflecting upon his original profession as a clergyman. But with men of better minds, it was a ground for their respect and confidence. And while the best friends of Mr. Everett would not claim for him what is more than human, an entire immunity from errors of judgment, they may safely challenge the proof of an act of his life, in violation of the principles of Christian ethics, which he always and everywhere eloquently taught to others.

The controlling influence of religious and Christian motives in the case of Mr. Everett, has been strikingly manifested in the last years of his life. What but such motives could induce the gerat labor of saving and dedicating to the memory of the father of his country, that most befitting monument, the acres he so much cherished in life at Mount Vernon? What but such motives could so deeply move his sympathies for his suffering countrymen of East Tennessee? And what motives but those flowing from a Christian faith, strong enough to inspire the eloquent lips of a dying man, to plead for the sufferers of Savannah? Thus, cementing with a charity that

never faileth, the Union restored by our victorious arms ؛
and illustrating the brave and beautiful sentiment uttered
by Mr. Everett while yet a young man, that " nothing is
too great to be done which is founded on truth and
justice, and which is pursued with the meek and gentle
spirit of Christian love." *

Hon. Levi Lincoln spoke as follows : —

MR. PRESIDENT : The startling announcement of the
death of the Hon. Edward Everett has occasioned
a shock to this community, from which those who have
known him long and well have not yet been able to
recover the calmness of entire self-possession. To such
as were his seniors in years, and have, at any time, been
the companions of his social hours, or his associates in
offices of public service, the event comes with impressive
admonition of the limitation of all human powers, and the
transitoriness of opportunities for earthly usefulness and
distinction. But a few days since, I met him, as an
associate in the presidential electoral college of Massachusetts, at that time strong at least in his usual health,
earnest as ever in patriotic duty, confident in anticipation
of triumph and glory to the struggling nation, and
buoyant with the hope that he should himself live to
rejoice in the restored Union of the states, and the universal freedom, peace, and prosperity of the people.
Never was he more genial in himself, or more interesting and instructive to others, than after the labors of

* Speech at Washington in 1832, on the colonization and civilization of Africa.

the day, at the festive board which his own generous hospitality had spread. And now, the seal of the transmitted record of his official action, on that occasion, is not yet broken, at the seat of government, and he who was placed in honor at the head of the electoral body is no more of earth. So pass away the venerated and the loved from the scenes of their loftiest labors.

The character of Gov. Everett is not to be portrayed with thoughtless haste, or judged by the superficial views which the mere remembrance of brilliant qualities may present. With the richest intellectual endowment, extraordinary mental cultivation, and great aptitude for communication, he united a persistent labor in acquisition, a clearness of perception, a power of analysis and concentration, a profoundness of thought, and a considerate judgment, which constituted in his person, a combination of virtues and graces, rarely if ever excelled. His early life was that of a scholar and a thinker, his mature years were a continued harvest of the treasures of learning and wisdom, which time and study and experience garnered up. It will be the grateful office of some gifted biographer to present the life of Gov. Everett in all its attractiveness of erudite knowledge, scientific accomplishment, and forensic capability, with a power of reasoning most persuasive, and an eloquence captivating and irresistible.

But it is of Gov. Everett in the relations to the offices of public employment and trust which he sustained and adorned, that it rather becomes me to speak. It has fallen to the lot of few men to fill so many and such

varied appointments of confidence and high responsibility.
His whole life was almost an unbroken public service.
The ministry to which he was first ordained, was but a
school of moral and Christian instruction and edification
to others.   In the university, whether as Professor or
President, he became the educator of the rising generation in the principles and virtues which are alike the foundation and the supports of a republican form of government.
In deliberative assemblies and the councils of state, his
eminent capacity and peculiar versatility and adaptation of
talent commended him to frequent demands for official
service, and he filled successively with distinguished
ability and conscientious fidelity, alike to his own great
honor and the approval of the country, the offices of
Representative in Congress, Governor of Massachusetts,
Secretary of State of the United States, and United States
Senator.   As minister to England, he sustained the dignity
and vindicated the rights of the nation, and happily
maintained, with signal success, its interest and its honor
intact, and unimpaired by the arts and designs of an
adverse diplomacy.   And yet more recently, in this last
great struggle for very existence, into which our once
united and prosperous country has been most wickedly
and deplorably plunged by plotting treason and flagrant
rebellion, who more loyally patriotic; who more efficiently active and influential in support of the Government and in defence of the Republic than Edward
Everett?   It may not be doubted that his words of
wondrous eloquence will do much, where even the missiles of war would be unheeded, to disabuse prejudice

and disarm hostility in the rebel states. The Mount Vernon fund, and the contributions to the relief of the Tennessee refugees, emphatically and *almost exclusively* collections of his unsurpassed sympathy and generosity and the persistent influence of a noble heart, with his last stirring utterances in aid of the beneficence of his fellow-citizens to the famishing people of repentant Savannah, proclaim him foremost among the benefactors of his country and the age.

I will not even attempt, Mr. President, to fill in the altogether too imperfect and hasty outline which I have sketched of the public services of this illustrious American citizen. His long life has been a blessing to mankind. The civilized world will deplore his death. His name and fame will be immortal.

Hon. Henry Chapin made the following remarks : —

Mr. President: It is eminently appropriate that the members of this Society should pay their tribute of respect to their late distinguished associate, and former president. By his pure life, his ripe scholarship, his varied acquirements, and his peculiar oratorical power, he reflected honor upon every association with which he was connected. In all these relations may be most appropriately applied to him the compliment once given to another, " *Nullum quod tetigit non ornavit.*"

In certain respects Edward Everett was a very remarkable man. His classic head and face, his elegant form, his singularly musical voice, his purity and strength of diction and his unsurpassed eloquence of speech will not be soon forgotten by any who have had the privilege to observe them. I never enjoyed the pleasure of his personal acquaintance. Indeed the idea of seeking it never occurred to me, but I looked upon his grace of action, and drank in his eloquent utterances, with unabated interest and constant admiration. On all occasions he was a gentleman, and at all times he bore himself with a quiet dignity, which was always fit and appropriate. A scholar, an orator, a patriot, and a Christian, he has filled a place in the country which no man now living can fill, and he will long be remembered by those who have listened to his words as one of the best models of scholarly eloquence and beautiful thoughts.

An instance of the effect of one of his masterly appeals will never be forgotten by me. It was on the occasion of the reception of the representatives of the Sacs and Foxes at Faneuil Hall. The Hall was filled to its utmost capacity, and many of course were excluded from entering it. Upon the arrival of the red men, the audience seemed moved as by some invisible demon of tumult and confusion. It swayed frightfully in every direction. The officers of the law seemed to .exert themselves in vain, and every one who was in a position to observe the surging mass looked upon it with feelings of anxiety, if not of dismay. In the midst of the tumult, Gov. Everett arose upon the platform, and his clear sweet voice sounded through the Hall with a magical and resistless power. Said he, " Gentlemen, suffer me to make an appeal to you." The rest of his language I am unable to recall, but in words firm, tender, and persuasive, he spoke of these untutored children of the forest, coming to the land of civilization and refinement, and he besought his fellow citizens so to demean themselves, that those who had never enjoyed the blessings and privileges which we enjoy, should carry home with them an exalted idea of their beneficent and purifying influence. Before he had half completed his remarks, the tumult had subsided, and at the close of his appeal that mass of human beings stood as quiet and still as the marble statues by his side.

I never before nor since beheld a more wonderful exhibition of the power of the human voice, and I remember no speech of his which to me was more eloquent or effective.

At times the speeches and writings of Mr. Everett, beautiful, eloquent, and polished though they are, often failed to reach the hearts of his hearers. The fault, perhaps, was either in his temperament, or in his cautious views upon the topics of the day, which at times almost gave the impression that he lacked depth of conviction. He was naturally timid and distrustful of change. He was the eloquent outgrowth of an age of compromise and expediency, and he presented all there was of that age to respect, in its most beautiful and attractive form. He revered the past, but distrusted the future. He believed in facts, but lacked faith in the power of ideas. He honored precedents, but doubted theories. He seemed at times almost to reverence expediency at the expense of absolute right. He was the eloquent expositor of the past, the beautiful delineator of the present, but he was not the bold prophet of

the future.   Hence during the vigor of his life, impressed
with an honest fear of evils to come, he seemed to throw
his transcendent talents in the way of progress and reform,
until he was almost crushed beneath their advancing tread,
and the lovers of liberty and right had almost come to
look upon him as an enemy to freedom and humanity.
Blessed be God, the veil lifted at last from his vision.
The first gun which was fired at Fort Sumter drove the
warm blood to his heart; with true manliness and magnanimity he declared that he had been mistaken, and he
girded himself for the conflict.   No service during these
years of war has been shunned, no duty has been neglected by him.   Throwing both head and heart into the
great struggle for free institutions, he has redeemed himself in the minds and hearts of his contemporaries, he
has demonstrated to the world his integrity and patriotism, and he has placed his name high on the scroll of the
friends of the country, and the defenders of the rights of
man.   He died at the zenith of his true fame, his last
days were his best, and the tears of a grateful people do
justice to his memory and to his great and patriotic
services.

MEMORIAL SERVICES

AT THE

EVERETT SCHOOL.

MEMORIAL SERVICES AT THE EVERETT SCHOOL.

On the morning of Saturday, January 21, 1865, at nine o'clock, the scholars of the Everett School were assembled in the spacious hall of the Schoolhouse, on Northampton Street. The Committee of the School were present, and a large number of the parents of the children. The Master of the School, Mr. George B. Hyde, commenced the exercises by reading appropriate selections from the Scriptures. Prayer was offered by Rev. Robert C. Waterston, after which a hymn was sung by the members of the first class.

Alden Speare, Esq. Chairman of the Sub-Committee, then stated the purposes of the present gathering, setting forth the loss this school had sustained in the death of Mr. Everett, and the multitude of reasons which impelled us to pay respect to his memory. He closed by introducing Frederic F. Thayer, Esq. who, as Chairman of the Sub-Committee of the School for the year 1860, was familiar with all the circumstances connected with the naming and the dedication of the Schoolhouse.

Mr. Thayer spoke as follows : —

Mr. Chairman: When, yesterday, I received your kind invitation to be present here this morning, and to say a few words, I confess to mingled emotions of gratitude for the compliment of the invitation; and of conscious inability to say anything worthy of the occasion. But inasmuch as here I am not a stranger, and lest my silence might be construed to indicate a diminution of interest in this School, or an indifference to the occasion, I shall venture to occupy a few moments of the hour, set apart for this sad memorial service.

We have reached the last day of a week of mourning. On its first morning, when all the Christian world was preparing for the quiet of another Sabbath, the foremost man among us was called from the turmoils and excitements of earth to his everlasting rest. From the crowd who were accustomed to go to the house of God in company, one was missing; our hope and our faith prompt the suggestion, that another had joined the society of "the spirits of just men made perfect." A mortal, though loved, honored as few men ever have been, yet a mortal, by one of the kindliest agencies, through which the angel of death visits human habitations to execute his terrible mission, had laid aside the burden of the flesh, with its anxieties, its struggles, and its sorrows, and put on the immortal vestments, with the emblematic palm-wreath and crown. And as the voice of the Christian minister was lifted to lead the devotions of his people in prayer to God, for the forgiveness of their sins, in thankfulness for innumerable blessings, it did not fail to offer also the petition of a whole people, stricken by sudden and overwhelming grief. From that day to this, has the prayer been repeated aloud in the busy marts of commerce, and in the privacy of a thousand homes, indicating so sincerely, an expression of bereavement so general, as almost never to have been equalled in the event of the death of any citizen.   The eloquence of the most gifted, the learning of the schools, and the heartfelt utterances of friend to friend, have indicated a realizing sense of the loss our city, our state, our country, the enlightened world, have sustained in his death, whose virtues, whose patriotism, whose learning, all vie with each other most fittingly to exalt and to commemorate.

Impelled by the same motives which have induced the numerous societies and associations, of which he was a member, to assemble that they might properly call to mind his pleasant connection with them, — to be experienced no more on earth, — and to make a respectful record to his memory, are we now assembled, — the teachers, the pupils, the Committee, and a portion of the friends of the Everett School ; to repeat in great measure, it may be, what others have said before us ; but on this spot, amid these scenes, wherein he was wont to join us with pleasure, — in this building, which is to bear his name, — probably when all of us, like him, have passed from earth, is to bear his name to the generations that shall be, until brick and stone, and mortar shall have crumbled, and the action of the elements shall have worn away from the tablet all traces of the letters which compose the illustrious name, — in this building, within these walls, resonant with his praise, and tributary of the esteem, with which the men of this generation regarded him, we do gratify our feelings of reverence and of affection, as we gather here in sympathy with a whole community; and among ourselves, in our own way, to mourn for the lamented dead, where we have met to rejoice with the honored living.

I am aware, Mr. Chairman, that I am indebted for the compliment of an invitation to be present on this occasion to the fact, that a few years since, it was my privilege to bear an humble part in connecting Mr. Everett's name permanently with this school.

To a gentleman, now a member of the Committee, and myself, were entrusted the arrangements for the dedication, and we entered upon our duties, by waiting upon Mr. Everett, to inform him of the action of the Board, and to request his presence at the dedication, which was to take place on the following Monday, the 17th of September, the 230th birthday of our city. He cheerfully complied with our request, and most of us remember with pleasure, his participation in the exercises of that day, when with his friends, the Hon. Robert C. Winthrop, President Felton, of blessed memory, Rev. Dr. George Putnam, of our neighboring city, and Rev. Dr. Eliot, of Washington University, he joined the city authorities, and teachers and pupils of the school, in consecrating this building to the lofty purposes of education, — under his revered name, to hold no unworthy place among the excellent schools of our metropolis.

That Mr. Everett appreciated what had been accomplished, in this appropriation of his name, we may learn, if we recall the words used by him, on that occasion, where he says, " Devoted, for a pretty long life, to the public service, in a variety of pursuits and occupations, laboring, I know, I may say diligently, and I hope I may add, though sometimes with erring judgment, yet always with honest purpose, for the public good at home and abroad; I frankly own, sir, that no public honor, compliment, or reward which has fallen to my lot, has given me greater pleasure than the association of my name with one of these noble public schools of Boston." In full accordance with this expression, are other indications which have come under my personal observation. Both by letter, and from his own lips, have I had repeated assurance that he was deeply interested in the prosperity of this school; that he felt a just pride in its reputation and in its usefulness; and as he more than once said, he only waited the time, when his country could be relieved from threatening perils, to manifest his interest more by his frequent presence. Alas, for the school, that day will not come! Alas! for us and for the school, the demands of a bleeding country upon his patriotic services prevented his frequent and valuable participation in cultivating here the arts of peace. But thanks to the Providence which ordained it, he was found equal to the emergency, and in the hour of our country's greatest need, when the hearts of men were failing them from fear, he stood forth, loftiest among the mighty, the safe counsellor, the champion of republican institutions in their purity, the intelligent and eloquent prophet of the ultimate triumph of liberty. You, my young friends of the school, were deprived of his benedictive presence and his valuable counsels; but his strength of body and mind, and the earnest prayers of his trusting, Christian heart were given to his country, which needed them more than you. And, to-day, when we are met to mourn his sudden departure, we can rejoice, that by the sublime efforts of his genius, as developed so recently in untried channels, and the consecration of his matchless powers to sustain all that is good in the institutions under which we live; in the outpourings of his lips that the hungry might be fed, the naked clothed, and the famishing restored; and all this, while not entirely neglecting the multitude of obligations which had claimed a share in his regards and his services, under a happier condition of national affairs, he showed to us and to the whole world that his last days were his best days, and every day as it came, shortening his career upon the earth, found him better fitted for heaven.

We can then, and we will mingle gratitude with our lamentations over his grave, — gratitude to God, that to our times he gave such a complete development of the highest manhood. We will be grateful for his services to the world, — grateful that his unsurpassed talents were never used but for the public good, — grateful that before our bodily eyes has been presented, in attractive form and feature, such an excellent example. In the refined scholar, in the accomplished orator, in the consummate statesman, in the perfect gentleman, in the unostentatious Christian, we find an embodiment of what our free institutions, in their highest culture, directed and controlled by a living Christianity, will produce. We will be grateful also for our humble connection with him, trifling though it be; for so much as it is, it has been another bond to whatever is good, and noble, and true. Whenever he has been with us, he did not leave us without his blessing. And now that he has ascended, I would that all which is worthy of remembrance and imitation, — and how much was there in such a life as his, — I would that it should be transfigured before us. As we shall see his living face no more, I rejoice that the devotion of the master of this school, and his reverence for him who was worthiest among the living, now sainted among the dead, prompted his generous heart to secure this splendid marble bust, calm, graceful, majestic, like him whose lineaments it so accurately portrays, but to-day decorated with the emblems of sadness, in sympathy with all around. I rejoice it is here. I rejoice it is to remain here, to be more precious than before; to remind all who enter within these walls that the ·presiding genius here is excellence, — excellence in conversation, excellence in deportment, excellence in intellectual accomplishments, excellence in Christian graces. Under such a tutelage, with the throng of coöperating advantages here enjoyed, we might trust in the most flattering promise of a generation of well educated, well balanced, firm principled, devoted, Christian women, to bear 'their honorable part in the great future of our country.

But, Mr. Chairman and friends, I have consumed the portion of time which it becomes me to occupy; and I must close, although I have just reached that part of my theme which most attracts me. I must leave to others to dwell upon the value of such an example before the youth of our land. What a wealth of beneficent influence is treasured up in the story of his life! Though " being dead, he yet speaketh." To all alike, young and old, he speaks, telling of the possibilities wrapped up in this nature of ours, of the responsibilities which accompany exalted talents, and how religiously they may be fulfilled; — of the present reward, which waits upon fidelity to duty, and a compliance with the providential directions of passing life, — telling, how it is possible to be great and good; to be kind, and virtuous, and true; to be learned in all worldly lore, to hold the loftiest positions among men, and yet be studious of the precepts of the Master, humbly following Him who " went about doing good,"— how it is possible to move uncontaminated amid the world's glittering fascinations and its fleeting shadows, — to turn aside from the broad highway and its sure destruction, to enter in at the straight gate, — to attain, as he attained, and to share with him " the peace and the progress of the skies."

Rev. R. C. Waterston, a member of the Sub-Committee, said : —

It is natural that we should strive to recall, as far as possible, each incident in the life of the illustrious benefactor who has been so recently taken from us. Every look and word, all the expressions of counsel and encouragement which we have heard him utter.

It was one of his great pleasures to visit this school,

bearing as it did his name; and you, I am quite sure, always felt it a privilege to welcome him.

In that volume from which we have just heard such appropriate passages read, — we are told that when Peter was in a certain city of Judea, one who had been actively useful, had been suddenly taken away. When the Apostle met the sorrowing company, they gathered around, showing the garments they had received, while the friend now departed was yet living. What a graphic touch of nature is that!

The instructive prompting of their hearts led them to recall those grateful reminiscences. It was the finest tribute which could be paid, surpassing in its simplicity all human eloquence.

Thus Shakespeare, with his transcendent knowledge of human nature, makes Mark Antony exclaim over the body of Julius Cæsar : —

> " You all do know this mantle, I remember
> The first time ever Cæsar put it on."

So in the presence of the Apostle, the people gather about him holding up for his notice the treasured memorials of their departed friend, recounting each act of kindness.

True to the same natural impulse, at the present moment, societies, associations, and individuals are meeting together, that they may express those feelings of respect and affection which gush up with fresh intensity in the heart. Fondly do they dwell upon each pleasant remembrance. What he has said and done in their behalf. The University, the City, the State, the Nation, pauses to recount every word and deed.

Ay, even while we speak, the steamer that so lately left this port, may be entering the harbor of Savannah, while those who receive the aid which has been thus generously sent, having heard already by the swift telegraph, of this sad event, may exclaim — "That eloquent voice (to be heard no more) gave forth its closing accents in our behalf. That which we receive, in this hour of need, comes as from his hand!"

So also with us, my young friends, we shall do well to recall in this impressive hour, whatever we may have known of that life and character. If we have seen that face, if we have heard that voice, if we have had any special opportunity at any time or in any way of becoming acquainted with a mind which exerted so wide and so powerful an influence, let us dwell upon it in thought, let us speak of it frankly one with another.

Thus if you remember Mr. Everett's visits to this School, if you can recall any of his remarks, you will do well to retain that recollection as vividly as possible; to strengthen the impression, and to add to its value by speaking of it to others.

I know that he gave a book to each of the older scholars, the name written out in connection with his own; with what constantly increasing interest, will others look upon that autograph!

My personal acquaintance with Mr. Everett commenced in 1834, — thirty-one years ago. I had written an article

for the North American Review, of which he was, at that
time, the editor.   He resided at Charlestown, and sent an
invitation for me to come and see him.   Never can I forget his kindness upon that occasion, a kindness which
knew no shadow through thirty years.   Within three
days of his death, I received two notes from him, in one
of which he says " I rise from my bed (to which I have
been mostly confined since Monday) to write you."   The
day following he says — " I was too ill to write at any
length yesterday, and I am not much better to-day."
Then, having added a few lines, he closes with the words
" My head is too cloudy."   A startling expression from
him, and, I confess, awakening the first feeling of apprehension.

This I received on Friday.   On Sunday morning he
was no more here.   On that Monday, to which he refers,
he had made his thrilling, and (as we then little knew)
his last speech at Faneuil Hall.   That mind which seemed
never cloudy before, had this slight foreshadowing, this
gentle intimation of the swift-approaching event.   Now,
even that momentary veil has been withdrawn, and that
mind, with its wonderful powers, has risen into celestial
glory.

How mysterious ! and yet is it not blended with grandeur ?   With every faculty in unsurpassed vigor, active
and useful, never more so, to the whole community and
the entire Nation, suddenly he is uplifted above the things
of time.   Sorrowful as we may feel, is there not reason
on his account for exultation ?

As long as the oldest of us here can remember, he has
36

been one of the most marked men of the country, and never has he been more honored or beloved than within the last four years of our country's strife and struggle.

Through these days of calamity and cloud, he has been firm and fearless. I need not dwell upon that patriotic devotion which we have all witnessed, and to which we shall ever recur with gratitude and delight.

My purpose at this time will be, not to dwell upon his public career, but briefly to consider two or three of those characteristics, which it may be of advantage for the pupils of this school, and for the young generally, to keep in mind.

The first characteristic to which I will refer is, his COURTESY. This, I believe, he extended at all times, to all persons, old and young, learned and ignorant, rich and poor. I doubt if he was ever guilty of a discourteous act to the least influential person, or even to an opponent. It is my conviction that this was in him no empty formality; but that it was based upon a thoughtfulness of the feelings and the rights of others. This respectfulness of manner, this grace of deportment, so marked, and so attractive in our distinguished friend, was a trait which the young may well keep before them as an incentive. Some things are beyond our reach, but this, to a considerable degree, is within the attainment of all.

At times, unawares, perhaps, the young acquire a brusk manner. They become, it may be, abrupt, hasty, pert, overbearing. They are not properly respectful to the aged. There is a lack of gentleness in their daily intercourse with their companions.

In what striking contrast to this was the manner and the spirit of Edward Everett.

Let the young, when they recall the splendor of those gifts which made him illustrious, and some of which are far beyond common acquirement, remember this winning and admirable trait, by which he imparted pleasure to many, through all the daily routine of life.

Another remarkable characteristic of Mr. Everett was his MEMORY.

This was no doubt in him a rare natural endowment. Still it was strengthened by care and culture. Probably no man in this country has possessed this faculty and perfected it to such a degree, unless it was John Quincy Adams; but this gift in him, though as extraordinary in some respects, was less marvellous in others.

John Quincy Adams appeared to remember the name of every person he had ever known, the ideas of every book he had ever read, and each fact which had ever presented itself to his knowledge. And, moreover, he was never at a loss. The instant that any subject was suggested, at that instant all his recollections and acquisitions were before him, in perfect order and ready for use. But with him, as far as I know, it was principally names, facts, data, the rich ore which he could work abundantly, and turn evermore to his purpose. All history and literature seemed familiar to his mind, his eye penetrating through everything at a glance, and resting upon the very fact he needed. But Mr. Everett, while he remembered facts, names, and data, could also recall with unerring exactness the precise language of an author.

We all know how he could with ease repeat, word for word, orations of one and two hours in length, without the slightest reference to notes, and this in a natural tone, without apparent effort, as if every expression was the spontaneous utterance of the moment.

I will mention a little incident illustrative of his memory, which happened to come within my knowledge. A friend of mine in London stated to me that an English gentleman, having printed a history of one of the interior counties of England, he sent a copy of the work to our city Library. In writing to Mr. Everett, as one of the Trustees of the Library, my friend suggested that, as the book was privately printed, it would doubtless be a gratification to the author if he should receive some special acknowledgment.

By the next steamer a letter was received from Mr. Everett — not only expressing thanks for the volume, but Mr. Everett stated in addition that he was at Oxford when that gentleman received his degree. That he listened with great pleasure to a Poem which that gentleman recited at that time, and that he was particularly impressed by the following lines. Here he quoted a passage from a Poem which had never been published, and which Mr. Everett heard incidentally from a young man at that time quite unknown, and in connection with the various public exercises of a Literary Festival, and yet years after he could recall those lines, and send them across the Atlantic to the author, who was as much astonished as if he had heard a voice coming down to him from the heavens.

It is doubtful if there is another man in the country

who could have exercised such a singular power of memory, or have made such a felicitous use of it.

Mr. Everett's natural gift he used and directed with consummate care. It would be curious to know more fully his rules and practices. While at College he committed the whole of Locke on the Human Understanding, so that he could repeat it word for word, from the introduction to the close. And in an address delivered at the request of the Massachusetts Historical Society, I heard him repeat more than one hundred and eighty names of authors and artists of different nations, Greek, Latin, German, Italian, Spanish, French, in exact order, with as much apparent ease as he would have spoken his own name.

This power varies in different persons, but there is no faculty more perceptibly affected by culture. You may be sure, my young friends, that by every lesson you learn, by every paragraph you commit, you are strengthening this important faculty of mind, which may prove an incalculable advantage to you in after life. No one can fully estimate the value of this faculty to such a man as Mr. Everett. How different he would have been with that one power wanting! And how greatly is the world indebted to him for the diligence and wisdom with which he employed it.

The next and closing characteristic of which I will speak is that fidelity which was manifested by Mr. Everett, not only in great but in minor duties. It was said of Oberlin that he was conscientious even to the rounding of an O. Mr. Everett was faithful to the same degree.

Nothing was too minute for his observation or his care. You see it in every note he penned, in every word he uttered. It mattered not whether he was to give an elaborate oration before some learned University, or a brief address before some small Society, or simply a remark to an individual, the words to be spoken were well considered. There was an appropriateness and a completeness which made it memorable.

Every pamphlet he received he acknowledged with his own hand, and whatever he did was done promptly. His industry and punctuality were something extraordinary. The notes from which I have quoted, received within three days of his death, are a proof that not even illness could prevent him from fulfilling, even to within a few hours of his departure, whatever it was within his power to do. I confess that even more than for his most splendid achievements do I honor him for his life-long fidelity to the minutest of duties. These were the steps by which he climbed to surprising elevations. The rounds in that ladder, which, planted on the earth, reached upward and upward. Every young person may learn a lesson of wisdom from Mr. Everett here. Wordsworth tells us that —

> " The primal duties shine aloft — like stars ;
> The charities that soothe, and heal, and bless,
> Are scattered at the feet of man — like flowers."

So there were gifts in Mr. Everett which we may never aspire to possess. They shine aloft like stars, to cheer and guide us in our pathway; but there are qualities which are scattered bountifully within our reach. Let us then gain whatever advantage is possible from any portion of his life, and any characteristics of his mind, which may offer for us a lesson.

There are those who will remember Mr. Everett chiefly as the Orator; some will dwell upon him as the Statesman; some as the man of Letters; some will recall his patriotism in these latter days of his country's trial. But while you think of him as the Scholar, the Patriot, the Statesman, the Orator, — you will think of him, perhaps, most fondly as the friend of the Everett School. You will dwell upon him in thought, as he appeared to you while here. May his example inspire you to constant diligence, and may the memory of what he accomplished lead you to perpetual progress.

Mr. Charles W. Slack said : —

Mr. Chairman and Friends : Mr. Everett's character was so many-sided that there are few who cannot speak of some one particular quality that makes his memory and name respected. For me, two or three will suffice on this occasion.

1. His deep interest in public education. Himself a graduate at the age of 10 of the North (now Eliot) School of this city, his children severally educated, in part, at the public schools, and his every influence exerted for the success of the common-school system of our State, he was particularly near to us who meet on this occasion. As Governor of Massachusetts, he was largely influential in giving permanence to the beneficial system of Normal

Schools, which are alike our pride and strength. True, Horace Mann was a potential coadjutor in this good work of a systematic and progressive scheme of School education, but Mr. Everett gave the large weight of his official and personal aid to the work. Then, also, he was largely the promoter of the lyceum or lecture system, now so common and so popular. Before his day, the lecture-course for the instruction of the people was wholly unknown. How much we are indebted to him for this great service, we can readily appreciate should we be deprived of our Mercantile Library, our Parker-Fraternity, our Young Men's Christian Association's Lectures, or, more recently, those charming lectures of Mr. Emerson, all of which are the direct result of Mr. Everett's desire to instruct and benefit the community. Surely, we can all thank him for these educational advantages to the common people.

2. His wonderful and systematic industry, joined with a courteous readiness to aid in any proper work for the benefit of his fellow-citizens. Think of his long and varied life! the tasks imposed upon him in each sphere, and with what rare fidelity he discharged his several trusts! What files of addresses, reports, messages, letters, orations, attest his knowledge, scholarship, coöperation, as well as eloquence! He was ever a cheerful worker. I think no one ever appealed to him for assistance in a laudable enterprise that did not, if he were not pre-occupied, receive it cordially and punctually. And this trait of his punctuality was a marked one. It was as much a charm of his life as his eloquence. He never de-

layed, even in the minutest, and, seemingly, most unimportant particulars. I remember, last September, being interested in a meeting in Faneuil Hall, to have realized the value of this excellence. It was just after the brilliant success of the indomitable and persistent Sherman, who, amid the mountains of Georgia, had just planted his colors in triumph over the city of Atlanta. It was while the news was coming to us that the brave old Farragut had defiantly made the passage of the forts in Mobile Bay, and conquered the second city of the South without even placing his foot upon the land. Some of us wanted to celebrate these victories in Faneuil Hall. As one of the Committee of Arrangements, I called on Mr. Everett, to aid in its success. He received me cordially, thanked me heartily for the honor, told me his whole heart and soul was in response to the glad tidings and the objects of the meeting, but he had for a few days been very feeble in health, was busily engaged in the preparation of twelve lectures upon law for Harvard University, there was scarce time for him to elaborate a first-class oration for the occasion, as he should desire, and, very reluctantly, he must decline the invitation. To assent cheerfully to the disappointment, for such reasons, was only a duty. "But you can send a letter, Mr. Everett, to the meeting, can you not?" I asked. "With great pleasure," was the cordial response, "if that will be acceptable. Call to-morrow at four o'clock, and it shall be ready for you." I need not say that at the hour named, almost to a minute, that letter was in my hands, in his well-known, faultless chirography, no interlineations, every *t* crossed, every *i* dotted, — a model for teacher or pupil in any school; and this from a man pressed with untold cares, and in the seventy-first year of his age! That letter I have now with me, just as it was prepared for that rejoicing Faneuil Hall assembly by Mr. Everett himself. I have been solicited by committees of national fairs, lovers of choice autographs, and others, to part with it. What committees and friends could not by entreaty and long persuasion induce me to surrender, I now cheerfully give to the Everett School, through its Principal, to be added to such other *souvenirs* as may be possessed, as my tribute, as a past chairman and a past secretary of the Everett School District Committee, to the memory of a man deserving to have the School named in his honor.

3. His Nationality. This was deep-seated, far-reaching, wholly American. He believed in the American name, American literature, science, commerce, manufactures, and the craft of the artisan. Never was this quality so brilliantly illustrated as during the last four years. American law, order, nationality, the sovereignty of a great people, the perpetuity of the great republic, were the themes which found expression in a hundred ways of popular address. He sustained the war, he sustained the government, he sustained the administration, it was all unselfish, disinterested, cordial, patriotic. No man can measure the value of this support — scarce one throughout the continent equalled it in influence. This memory of the departed will to many be the sweetest and longest enduring.

I fear, Mr. Chairman, I do not join with many in the

feeling of profound sorrow which has attended this departure.   I cannot divorce my mind from the thought that it
is a wise consummation of a full-measured and rounded-
out existence here.   To me it is in accord with the beneficent laws of nature.   I know that the wilting and falling
leaves of the flower only indicate that its keenest fragrance
and intensest coloring have been given to its admirers ; I
see the golden fruit, streaked with its ribands of emerald
and ruby, hanging in the autumn sun, and at the favoring
moment it drops, fully ripe, into the lap of mother earth ;
the dying swan, we are told, throws forth its sweetest
notes of song with its expiring breath ; and may we not
believe that, with the same all-wise provision for His
children, the good Father called our departed friend when
his work was fully done, his life wholly completed, and
his memory should be the sweetest to all who remain ?
Let us be thankful *we* have that memory, that life, that
work, and from them each shall radiate influences which
shall evermore bless and benefit the world.

The master of the School, in. a few appropriate remarks,
accepted the gift, and the exercises were closed by singing.

PROCEEDINGS AND RESOLUTIONS

VARIOUS ORGANIZATIONS.

OVERSEERS OF HARVARD COLLEGE.

Boston, January 26, 1865.

The following Preamble and Resolutions were prefaced with remarks by the Reverend James Walker, D. D., and presented to the Board : —

Whereas it has pleased God to take from this life the Hon. Edward Everett, a distinguished member of this Board ; therefore

Resolved, That we avail ourselves of the earliest opportunity to record our sense of the great loss which Harvard College has sustained in the death of one of the most illustrious of her sons.

Resolved, That, as one branch of the government of the college, we would especially acknowledge his early services to the University as Professor of Greek Literature, which were welcomed with so much enthusiasm by the scholars of that day, and did so much to give an impulse to classical learning in this country ; and also the unsurpassed dignity with which, in later life, he filled the office of President, his administration being marked by all his accustomed care and thoroughness, and only prevented by its brevity from becoming one of the most useful and brilliant the college has known.

Resolved, That, as members of this Board, we regret that we are no longer to be assisted in our deliberations by his wisdom and experience in college affairs, nor to have before us his example in the faithful discharge of every public trust, recommended by uniform courtesy.

Resolved, That we also sympathize in the general mourning for the death of a great and good man ; not forgetting in the eminent scholar, the enlightened states- man, or the conspicuous and revered citizen, — one whom Providence seemed to have raised up, in the troubled state of the country, to be of great influence in restoring union and peace.

Resolved, That the secretary be requested to transmit a copy of these resolutions to the family of Mr. Everett.

The Preamble and Resolutions were seconded in an appropriate address by Rev. Artemas B. Muzzey ; and after eulogistic remarks by His Excellency the Governor of the Commonwealth, President of the Board, and Philip H. Sears, Esq., Rev. James F. Clarke, D. D., David H. Mason, Esq., and Hon. Thomas Russell, they were adopted by a unanimous vote, the members rising from their seats, in token of affirmation.

Attest : NATH'L B. SHURTLEFF,
Secretary of the Overseers.

FACULTY OF HARVARD COLLEGE.

The following resolutions in honor of Mr. Everett were adopted by the Faculty of Harvard College, January 18, 1865 : —

Resolved, That we lament, in the death of Mr. Everett, the loss of a kind friend, an honorable citizen, a gifted, well-trained, and patriotic statesman, and a bright example of finished scholarship.

Resolved, That now, when another thread in the silver cord of living ex-presidents of the college has been loosed, we remember with gratitude and admiration the long and varied services of the departed to the college, as Student, Graduate, Professor, Governor, President, and Overseer.

Resolved, That as members of the Faculty of instruction and government, over which Mr. Everett formerly presided with unsurpassed dignity and gentleness, we delight to trace even now the beneficent influences of his too brief administration, as of a patient and watchful guardian, an inspiring scholar, and a Christian gentleman.

Resolved, That we accept the invitation of the Mayor of Boston to attend the funeral ceremonies in that city.

Cambridge, *January* 18, 1865.

STANDING COMMITTEE OF THE FIRST CHURCH.

BOSTON, January 17, 1865.

At an adjourned meeting of the Standing Committee of the First Church, held this day, with members of the congregation, G. W. Messinger, and S. L. Abbot, the Sub-Committee appointed for that purpose, submitted the following preamble and resolutions, which were unanimously adopted : —

Whereas, It has pleased the All-wise Disposer of events to remove from us, by sudden death, our esteemed fellow-worshipper and beloved friend EDWARD EVERETT, and,

Whereas, We wish to put on record an expression of our sense of the great private worth which distinguished him no less than his public virtues ; therefore, be it

Resolved, That, by his decease, the members of the First Church and congregation have lost one strongly endeared to them by the association which has bound them together as worshippers, for many years past.

Resolved, That we gratefully recall the constant interest which our departed friend took in the welfare of our venerable society ; an interest which he manifested to the last by his regular attendance on the offices of the Sanctuary.

Resolved, That we shall always hold his example in precious remembrance, as of one who, while he dignified our nation, especially in her hour of trial, by his unselfish patriotism, humanity, and generous devotion to the cause of republican liberty, was no less distinguished for the humility, purity, and Christian excellence of his private life.

Resolved, That these resolutions be placed on the records of the First Church, and that a copy be transmitted to the family of the deceased, with the assurance of our most tender sympathy in this hour of their heavy bereavement.

It was then

Voted, That Thomas B. Wales, Otis Rich, Samuel L. Abbot, Nathaniel Thayer, George W. Messinger, John Collamore, D. W. Salisbury, Edward Austin, J. Putnam Bradlee, Turner Sargent, George W. Wales, Edward Frothingham, George O. Shattuck, Joseph L. Henshaw, and Samuel H. Gookin of the congregation, be a committee to superintend the arrangements at the church during the funeral services of the late Edward Everett, and to confer with the committee of the City Government in the matters relating to the same.

The meeting was then adjourned *sine die*.

THOMAS B. WALES, *Chairman.*

GEORGE O. HARRIS, *Secretary.*

FRANKLIN MEDAL ASSOCIATION.

Pursuant to a call in the newspapers, the Association of Franklin
Medal Scholars met in the Mercantile Building, Summer Street,
on the morning of January 19, to take measures in honor of the
memory of their late President, — Hon. Edward Everett. Dr.
M. W. Weld was chosen Chairman.

The following resolutions were offered by Mr. Thomas Gaffield : —

Whereas, It hath pleased God to remove by the hand of the
of death our late President, Edward Everett :

Resolved, That while we unite with the head of the
nation, and with the legislative assemblies of the city, the
state, and the country, in mourning the loss of the patriot
and statesman ; with the lovers of liberty throughout the
world, in lamenting the departure of one of its noblest
champions, who, in the hour of his country's trial, came
up so gloriously to the defence of freedom and right, and
to the support of the Government and its defenders on the
land and on the sea ; we especially deplore the loss of
one who was the great American scholar ; one whom we
rejoice to know was nurtured in his youth in those public
schools, which are the honor of our city and our Com-

monwealth; who at the early age of ten years, received the Franklin prize for superior scholarship at the North School, and at the age of twelve, a similar token at the Latin School; whose career of superiority and excellence in scholarship followed him throughout his college course, and made him at an early period of life, take rank among the best writers and the most accomplished orators of the land, and placed him at a later age at the head of that University which he always loved, and which always delighted to honor its most distinguished graduate.

Resolved, That as graduates of our Public Schools, in which, as in all educational institutions, he took so deep an interest to the last year of his life, we gratefully revere the memory of the departed scholar, statesman, and patriot, and heartily commend to the youth of our city and our country, the study of his writings, so full of wisdom and learning, and the imitation of his life, so crowned with the fruits of literary industry, with the deeds of noble patriotism, and the works of true Christian benevolence.

Resolved, That we most deeply sympathize with the family of the deceased, and reverently point them to the consolations of that Gospel, which he so earnestly and eloquently set forth in the days of his early manhood.

Resolved, That the members of this Association attend the funeral services at the First Church in Chauncy Street, this day.

Resolved, That a copy of the above resolutions be transmitted by the secretary to the family of the deceased.

After remarks by Messrs. Gaffield, Stetson, Harris, and Pratt, the resolutions were unanimously adopted.

Mr. Gaffield then offered the following, which were also unanimously adopted : —

Resolved, That while the memory of Edward Everett will ever be enshrined in the hearts of his countrymen, and while the words and the deeds of his life will constitute his noblest monument, we cordially unite with our fellow-citizens in any.movement to honor his worth and commemorate his name.

Resolved, That we heartily approve of the proposition to erect a statue to his memory, and direct that our treasurer pay over to the committee appointed for the purpose at Faneuil Hall, on the 18th inst., the sum of one thousand dollars, as the subscription of the Association of Franklin Medal Scholars. ·

It was moved that a committee of five be appointed by the chair to represent this Association at the church. The motion was adopted, and the following-named gentlemen were appointed, viz : Isaac Harris, Thomas Gaffield, S. F. Smith, J. C. Pratt, T. W. Gould.

The meeting then dissolved.

MERCANTILE LIBRARY ASSOCIATION.

At a special meeting of the Mercantile Library Association of Boston, held on Wednesday evening, January 18, 1865, the following Resolutions were offered by Charles H. Frothingham, and were unanimously adopted : —

Whereas, It has pleased Almighty God to remove from us by death our late eminent and illustrious citizen, Edward Everett, whose loss is justly regarded as a national calamity, and strikes with unspeakable sorrow this community in which he had so long lived; we, the members of the Mercantile Library Association of Boston, to whom he was a near neighbor and sincere friend and benefactor, desiring to express our affectionate regard for his memory, unanimously adopt the following resolutions : —

Resolved, That we are profoundly grateful to Divine Providence for his long life filled with honor to himself and his country; for his death without suffering, and for his possession of all his glorious faculties to the last, unimpaired; and, while humbly submitting to the inscrutable decree of the Great Disposer of events, we cannot but deplore the loss to American literature and oratory of their brightest ornament, and to the Union of its warmest advocate, whose exalted character, and lofty, disinterested patriotism would have exerted an influence, at home and abroad, more potent than any other citizen, in the final settlement of our existing difficulties.

Resolved, That we will remember that he was as good as he was great, and as amiable as he was accomplished. Like Washington, whom it was his privilege to hold up to his admiring fellow-countrymen, he possessed that rare combination of qualities which constitutes an evenly balanced mind. Always magnanimous in heart and action, in justice to man and in obedience to God, he ever showed those qualities of grace and loveliness which denote the true Christian gentleman; and especially thankful are we for those last words in favor of " Christian retaliation " at the meeting in aid of the suffering poor of Savannah.

Resolved, That while we contemplate the noble portrait of the Father of his Country, which he presented to us, and endeavor to hold dear the memory and revere the name and character of Washington, we will ever associate with that name that of our late distinguished benefactor, and we will proudly preserve his bust of which we are the fortunate possessors.

Resolved, That we will regard him as an example for our emulation of industry in every station; of refined culture, and of patriotic inspiration.

Resolved, That we tender to the family of the deceased our heartfelt sympathy and condolence in this season of their affliction, and as a further token of our respect and love for his memory we will attend his funeral.

A true copy of the record,

HENRY C. PYNE,
Recording Secretary.

FRANKLIN TYPOGRAPHICAL SOCIETY.

At the regular monthly meeting of the Franklin Typographical Society, on the evening of February 4, after the formal business had been transacted, the President alluded to the decease of Mr. Everett; and after referring to the great loss sustained by the whole country, recalled to notice the generous services which Mr. Everett rendered the Society five years previously, by delivering before them his address on the life and character of Benjamin Franklin. The funds of the Society had at that time become so reduced that it was much straitened in providing for the needs of its sick members; and Mr. Everett, on being applied to, cheerfully consented to deliver an address in behalf of its treasury, the committee of arrangements agreeing to give him the remuneration which he ordinarily received for such a service. When payment was tendered to him, after the address, Mr. Everett declined compensation, saying that since he made the engagement he had become more fully acquainted than before with the charitable objects of the Society, and that he had derived great satisfaction from addressing so intelligent a body of men, with whom, he remarked, he placed himself in magnetic sympathy more readily than with most audiences before which he was accustomed to appear. The President expressed his conviction that this act of benevolent kindness, on the part of Mr. Everett, had been of lasting benefit to the Society, by inducing men of wealth to regard its claims for aid, which they had previously overlooked.

When the President had concluded his remarks, Mr. Ambrose H. Goodridge moved that a committee of three be appointed by the Chair to report a series of resolutions, expressive of the sentiments of the members, in relation to the sad event to which allusion had been made. The Chair appointed as the Committee, Messrs. Goodridge, C. W. G. Mansfield, and James Cox, who subsequently reported the following series of resolutions, and they were unanimously adopted : —

Resolved, That in the recent decease of Edward Everett, the members of the Franklin Typographical Society, in common with the community in which he lived, and with the nation of whose history his life forms so important a part, feel that an irreparable loss has been sustained by every good and patriotic cause and institution in the country.

Resolved, That throughout the long and public career of the eminent statesman, whose demise we mourn, we recognize the qualities of rare goodness as well as exalted greatness, prompting him to acts of charity and benevolence, in which he engaged with unfaltering zeal.

Resolved, That we remember with abiding gratitude the timely and important aid which he rendered to our Society, a few years since, at a period when its means were greatly reduced, by his generous and voluntary labors in behalf of our charitable fund.

Resolved, That we tender to. the family and immediate friends of the deceased our profound sympathies in their bereavement.

Resolved, That the secretary be directed to transmit a copy of these resolutions to the family of the deceased, and that they be entered upon the records of the Society.

MASSACHUSETTS CHARITABLE MECHANICS' ASSOCIATION.

The Government of this Association held a special meeting on Tuesday, January 17, in the afternoon, to consider the death of Hon. Edward Everett, an honorary member. Joseph T. Bailey, Esq., President, announced the sad bereavement which had called the Trustees together; and Hon. Wm. W. Clapp, Jr. offered the following preamble and resolutions, which were unanimously adopted : —

The death of the Hon. Edward Everett having removed from our list of honorary members one, who for many years has given to us convincing proof of his interest in our Association, therefore

Resolved, That, in the death of Mr. Everett, we feel the loss of a prized friend, a wise counsellor, and an honored benefactor, whose intercourse with us has cheered and encouraged us, whose heart, constantly devoted to our good, has successfully manifested its sincerity in kindly acts, and whose gifted mind has ever sought our benefit; whose deep sympathy with mechanical pursuits and interest in the artisan have secured for him the gratitude and respect of the workingman; and whose associations with us we regard with proud satisfaction, enjoying as we did, so long, the invigorating influence of his massive character.

Resolved, That we will enter upon our records this mark of respect to the memory of Mr. Everett, who was held, while living, in the highest regard by every member of our Association.

Resolved, That the government will attend the funeral of Mr. Everett, with such members of the Association as wish to join with them in paying this tribute of respect.

BUNKER HILL MONUMENT ASSOCIATION.

A special meeting of the directors of the Bunker Hill Monument Association, was held on the 18th of January, in the Council Chamber, City Hall, to take suitable action upon the death of Hon. Edward Everett, who was one of the Vice-Presidents of the Association. His Honor Mayor Lincoln presided. The following resolutions were offered by W. W. Wheildon, Esq., and unanimously adopted by the meeting : —

Resolved, That the government of this Association have learned with deep emotion the death of their late associate, Edward Everett, whose services as its first secretary, as director and vice-president, for more than forty years, have been so generously and efficiently rendered, and whose advice, counsel, and transcendent talents have been so important in the promotion of the great object of its organization.

Resolved, That as an evidence of our respect for his unblemished character, of appreciation of his disinterested labors, of acknowledgment of his unvarying courtesy and kindness, and as a recognition of his patriotic devotion to his country, this Board will attend his funeral and participate in those honors so justly due to his distinguished abilities and his exalted worth.

Resolved, That the loss of one who was always ready and present when needed; who was equally good and great; who excelled all others in devotion and effort, and was constantly outdoing and overdoing himself, leaves an " aching void" which time itself may not fill.

> " Now he is gone! vainly and wearily
> Groans the full heart, the yearning sorrow flows —
> Gone! and all the zest of life in one long sigh,
> Goes with him where he goes."

Resolved, That a committee be appointed to express in suitable form that respect for his memory, that honor for his virtues, and that gratitude for his services, entertained by this Association, to be presented at its next annual meeting, and placed enduringly upon its records.

The following gentlemen were appointed to constitute the committee designated in the resolutions : —

R. C. Winthrop, W. W. Wheildon, J. Mason Warren, Albert Fearing, J. H. Thorndike, Benjamin T. Reed, Samuel H. Russell, Henry A Pierce, F. W. Lincoln, Jr., G. W. Warren.

Voted, That the Secretary notify the Chairman of the City Committee that the Directors will attend the funeral of Mr. Everett on the 19th instant; and that the members of the Association be requested to unite with them on the occasion.

The meeting was then dissolved.

Attest :   S. F. McCLEARY, *Secretary*.

LINCOLN GUARD.

At a meeting of the First Unattached Company of Infantry,
M. V. M. (Lincoln Guard), Capt. Moses E. Bigelow, at their
armory in South Boston, on Monday Evening, January 16, the
following resolutions were unanimously adopted : —

Whereas, Divine Providence, in his impartial dealings
with man, has, by the very sudden decease of the Hon.
Edward Everett, of this State and city, deprived this
country of one of its firmest friends, in this, her hour of
peril :

Resolved, That the members of this Company honor the
departed as one of the greatest statesmen of the age, as
a disinterested politician, and as a scholar and orator unequalled; and that we see in his long and successful
career, a bright incentive to do our duty well, leaving the
reward to the judgment of our fellow-men.

Resolved, That we, in common with the President of the
United States, and her more humble citizens, truly feel
that the country has sustained an irreparable loss, which
we deeply lament.

Resolved, That our commander be authorized to tender
the services of the Company, for military escort and fare-

well honors to the remains of this truly great man, to his
Honor the Mayor or such persons as have the funeral
obsequies in charge.

Resolved, That the flag be placed at half-mast on our
armory, until after the funeral.

EDWARD EVERETT.

Born at Dorchester, Mass. April 11, 1794.

Attended Village School in Dorchester, 1797.

Attended school in North Bennet Street, Boston, 1803.

Attended private school, Short Street, Boston, 1804.

Attended Public Latin School, Boston, 1805–06.

Prepared for College at Exeter Academy, 1807.

Entered Harvard College, 1807; graduated 1811.

Appointed Tutor of Latin at Harvard College, 1812.

Pastor of Brattle Street Church, 1813–14.

Published "Defence of Christianity," 1814,

Professor of Greek Literature at Harvard College, 1815–25.

Studied at University of Göttingen, 1816–17.

Degree of P. D. conferred at Göttingen, 1817.

Returned from Europe in 1819.

Editor of *North American Review*, 1820–23.

Delivered Phi Beta Kappa Oration, August, 26, 1824.

Member of Congress from 1825 to 1835.

Degree of LL. D. conferred at Yale College, 1833.

Degree of LL. D. conferred by Harvard College, 1835.

Governor of Massachusetts from 1836 to 1840.

Sailed for Europe, June, 1840.

Minister to the Court of St. James, 1841–44.

Degree of LL. D. conferred by University of Cambridge, England, 1842.

Degree of LL. D. conferred by Dublin University, Ireland, 1842.

Degree of J. C. D. conferred by University of Oxford, England, 1843.

President of Harvard College, 1846–1849.

Degree of LL. D. conferred by Dartmouth College, 1849.

Secretary of State of the United States, 1852.

Chosen President of the Board of Trustees Public Library, 1852.

United States Senator from Massachusetts, 1853.

Resigned Senatorship, May, 1855.

Oration on Washington (first time), February 22, 1856.

Nominated for the Vice-Presidency of United States, 1860.

Chairman of Commission on a Military Academy for Massachusetts, 1863.

Chosen Presidential Elector, 1864.

Address in aid of the citizens of Savannah, January 9, 1865.

Died in Boston, January 15, 1865.

Obsequies in Boston, January 19, 1865.

[He has spoken before the Municipal Authorities of Boston on the following occasions] :—

Boston Public School Examination, July 23, 1837.

Dinner in Faneuil Hall, July 4, 1838.

Railroad Jubilee, September 19, 1851.

Dinner to Thomas Baring, September 16, 1852.

Dinner in Faneuil Hall, July 4, 1853.

Boston School Festival, July 23, 1855.

Dedication of Public Library, January 1, 1858.

Dinner in honor of Mehemmed Pasha, May 25, 1858.

On the death of Rufus Choate, Faneuil Hall, July, 1859.

Eulogy on Daniel Webster, Music Hall, September 17, 1859.

Dinner to the Sanitary Convention, June, 1860.

Oration in Music Hall, July 4, 1860.

Dinner to officers of the Russian Fleet, June 7, 1864.

Reception of the officers and crew of the Kearsarge, November 10, 1864.

Printed in France by Amazon
Brétigny-sur-Orge, FR